S0-BFC-362

The Complete Guide to
Traditional Japanese Performing Arts

装幀 ● 菊地信義
装画 ● 野村俊夫

イラスト ● 高橋 満
編集協力 ● 翻訳情報センター

翻訳 ● 歌舞伎 …Sheryl Chow
　　　能・狂言 …Marc Shultz
　　　文楽 …Lucy North
　　　日本舞踊・落語・講談・浪曲 …Richard Sams

写真協力 ● 歌舞伎 …国立劇場 p.25「勧進帖」,
　　　　　　　p.44「助六曲輪菊」

　　　　　能・狂言 …国立能楽堂 p.115「敦盛」,
　　　　　　　p.116「井筒」, p.116「附子」

　　　　　文楽 …国立劇場 p.181「国性爺合戦」,
　　　　　　　p.194「仮名手本忠臣蔵」

　　　　　日本舞踊 …社団法人 日本舞踊協会
　　　　　　　p.249「鉄輪」

　　　　　落語・講談・浪曲 …横井洋司 p.249
　　　　　　　落語「柳屋小さん」、講談「宝井馬
　　　　　　　琴」、浪曲「玉川勝太郎」

DTPオペレーション ● (株) ポイントライン

Published by Kodansha International Ltd.,
17-14, Otowa 1-chome, Bunkyo-ku, Tokyo 112-8652.
No part of this publication may be reproduced
in any form or by any means without permission
in writing from the publisher.
Copyright © 2000 by Kodama Shōko
All rights reserved. Printed in Japan.

First Edition 2000

ISBN4-7700-2607-2
00 01 02　7 6 5 4 3 2 1

英語で話す「日本の伝統芸能」
The Complete Guide to
Traditional Japanese Performing Arts

小玉祥子

Bilingual Books

はじめに

「歌舞伎は旅する大使館」という言葉があります。

1978年、オーストラリアで歌舞伎の公演が行われ、中村歌右衛門らが参加して「義経千本桜」などを上演しましたが、シドニー・ヘラルド・モーニング紙の劇評は、「芸術の最高レベルに達している。まさに動く浮世絵。歌舞伎は旅する大使館だ」と、この公演を絶賛しました。それ以来、この言葉は歌舞伎の海外公演に際して使われるキャッチフレーズとなりました。

すばらしい芸術は、時に、外交に頼る以上に、国家や人種の壁を越えて人々の心を結びつけます。確かに「歌舞伎は旅する大使館」とはうまい表現です。歌舞伎だけではなく、文楽、能狂言も、外国公演で世界の人々に深い感動を与えています。文楽も能狂言も「旅する大使館」なのです。

この三つの伝統芸能を世界の人に理解してもらいたいと思ってまとめたのがこの本です。日本舞踊、そして、落語、講談、浪曲という大衆芸能も加えて、日本の伝統芸能の概要がわかるようにもしてみました。

日本独特の芸能の世界を言葉で説明することは困難で、十分に伝わりきれないところがたくさんあると思いますが、この本の解説をヒントに、皆さんがそれぞれの言葉で、日本の伝統芸能の姿を世界に伝えてほしいと思います。また、外国の方々の日本の伝統芸能理解の一助にもなれば幸いです。

小玉祥子

PREFACE

Kabuki has been called a traveling embassy.

In 1978, Nakamura Utaemon and his troupe performed the kabuki drama known as *Yoshitsune Senbon Zakura* in Australia. a critic from the *Sydney Herald Morning* praised it as an animated Ukiyoe world—the ultimate in art. He called kabuki "traveling embassy." From that time in this phrase has been as a slogan to describe overseas performance s of kabuki.

Magnificent art is often better than diplomacy at overcoming the walls of nation and race to bring people together. A traveling embassy is indeed an appropriate expression. Along with kabuki, *bunraku* puppet theater, nō plays and kyōgen comedies also serve as traveling embassies to those who see overseas performances of these arts.

This book is the result of my desire to further share these traditional performing arts with the world. I have also included Nihon-buyō Japanese dance, *rakugo* comic story telling, *kōdan* storytelling, and *rōkyoku* recitation—performing arts for the masses—to give the readers a broad picture of Japan's traditional arts.

It is indeed difficult to fully explain the world of Japanese art—words have their limits. I would, however, like readers to use this book as a reference source for sharing the Japanese arts in their own words. I would be most rewarded if this book contributes in some small way to the understanding of Japanese arts by those new to Japanese culture.

Kodama Shōko

目　次

CONTENTS

代表的な歌舞伎の作品

役者の役柄

REPRESENTATIVE KABUKI PLAYS

THE KABUKI ACTOR'S ROLE

舞台化粧と衣装

役者の演技と見せ場

歌舞伎の舞踊

KABUKI MUSIC

REPRESENTATIVE KABUKI PLAYWRIGHTS

KABUKI ACTORS AND THE YAGŌ

KABUKI ACTORS THEATER

能・狂言

能の始まりと発展

能の演目

演者の役割と能の構成

能の舞台

能の音楽

NŌ AND KYŌGEN

ORIGINS AND DEVELOPMENT OF NŌ

THE NŌ PERFORMANCE PROGRAM

THE STRUCTURE OF NŌ AND THE ACTORS' ROLES

THE NŌ STAGE

NŌ MUSIC

NŌ MASKS, COSTUMES, AND STAGE PROPERTIES

THE BASICS OF NŌ PERFORMANCE

THE WORLD OF THE NŌ ACTOR

KYŌGEN

文 楽

文楽の誕生と発展

文楽の作品と近松門左衛門

物語の構成と表現の特徴

義太夫節と三味線

人形と人形遣い

演者たちと文楽の興行

GIDAYŪ NARRATION AND SHAMISEN ACCOMPANIMENT

PUPPETS AND PUPPETEERS

BUNRAKU PLAYERS AND BUNRAKU PERFORMANCE

日本舞踊、落語、講談、浪曲

日本舞踊

落　語

講　談

浪　曲

NIHON BUYŌ, RAKUGO, KŌDAN, RŌKYOKU

NIHON BUYŌ (JAPANESE CLASSICAL DANCE)

RAKUGO

KŌDAN

RŌKYOKU

歌舞伎
Kabuki

歌舞伎のはじまり

 一口に言って、歌舞伎とはいったいどんなものですか。

A 歌舞伎は江戸時代初期に誕生した日本の伝統演劇です。庶民の中から生まれ、江戸幕府からの度々の弾圧にかかわらず、400年間に亘って愛されてきました。固定化することを嫌い、明治に至るまで、能、狂言、文楽など多くの芸能からおもしろいストーリーや演技様式などを取り込みながら、発展を続けました。

衣装などの色彩の美しさ、豪華な舞台や仕掛けなど、見所はいっぱいです。俳優の演技もその1つ。歌舞伎俳優は、日本ではトップクラスの演者たちですが、男性のみであることが大きな特徴です。ほとんどは少年期から修業を積みます。そして、女性の役に至るまで「女方」と呼ばれる男性が演じます。たゆまぬ鍛練の結果として、歌舞伎界からは時代を代表するような名優が次々と生まれ、最近では歌舞伎俳優が現代劇やミュージカル作品に出演する機会も増えています。

また、歌舞伎の演技様式は新劇や小劇場などの現代演劇にも強い影響を与えています。古典でありながら常に新しさを失わないのが歌舞伎なのです。

THE ORIGINS OF KABUKI

 What, briefly, is kabuki?

Kabuki is traditional theater that originated among the common people in the Edo period of Japan. Despite repression by the Edo shogunate, it managed to be popular for 400 years. The kabuki was able to avoid turning into a rigid, lifeless form; until the Meiji period, it continued to evolve by incorporating interesting narratives and performing styles from many other types of stage entertainment, such as nō, kyōgen, and bunraku.

There are so many aspects to kabuki that can be appreciated, such as brilliantly colored costumes, lavish staging, and brilliant stage devices. Last, but not least, are the technical skills of the kabuki actors, who number among the top in Japan. One feature of kabuki is that all its actors are men, most of whom begin their training at a very early age. All female parts are played by men called *onnagata* (female impersonator). Thanks to the unremitting training of its performers, the kabuki theater has given birth to great actors who have become a symbol of their age. And in recent years, greater opportunities have opened up for kabuki actors to appear in modern plays or musicals.

At the same time, the kabuki style of acting is exerting a strong influence on contemporary theater such as *shingeki*, or new-style theaters, and small-theater groups. Thus, although kabuki is a traditional art, it never loses its freshness of appeal.

Q 「歌舞伎」という名前はどのようにして
生まれて来たのですか。

A 漢字の「歌」は音楽、「舞」は踊り、「伎」
は演技という意味です。歌舞伎とはうまいネー
ミングですね。でも、これは実は当て字で
す。「歌舞伎」は元々は、動詞の「傾く」に
由来すると言われます。

豊臣秀吉(1536-98)の時代、派手な衣装を
着て町を歩く人々が出現しました。常識にと
らわれない彼らは、「常軌を逸した者」とい
う意味を込めて「傾き者」と呼ばれました。
その風俗を踊りに取り込んだのが歌舞伎の祖
とされる出雲(今の島根県)の阿国です。

16世紀の末に出雲大社の巫女と称する阿国
は京都に上り、神社の境内や四条河原などで
「ややこ踊り」(赤ちゃんのしぐさで踊る踊
り)、「念仏踊り」(太鼓や鉦などに合わせて、
念仏に節をつけてとなえがら踊る踊り) など
を踊って見せ、人気を博しました。

彼女の踊りは「かぶき踊り」と名付けられ
ました。やがて「かぶき」に「歌舞伎」の文
字が当てられるようになったわけです。

出雲の阿国

Q 歌舞伎は女性の役も男性が演じるそうですが、
いつから男性のみになったのでしょうか。

A やがて阿国は男装し、「傾き者」の姿を
して、茶屋女(茶屋で客の相手をする遊女)と
客がたわむれる様子などを踊りで見せるよう
になりました。この阿国の「かぶき踊り」の

Q How did the name *kabuki* come about?

The kanji (Chinese characters used in writing) for *ka* means "music," *bu* means "dance," and *ki*, "performance." As you can see, it's very aptly named. But in fact, the kanji were appropriated because they were the phonetic equivalents of the word *kabuki*, which is actually derived from the verb, *kabuku*.

During the time of Toyotomi Hideyoshi (1536–1598), people started showing up on streets dressed in outlandish fashion. These unconventional people were called *kabukimono*, or one who goes off the beaten path. This fashion was incorporated into a dance form by Okuni, a shrine maiden from Izumo (today's Shimane Prefecture), who is regarded as the founder of kabuki.

At the end of the 16th century, Okuni went to Kyōto, where she performed dances within shrine compounds and dry river beds of Shijo. Her dances, *yayako odori* (dancing with the gestures of infants) and *nenbutsuodori* (a prayer dance performed while chanting the sutra to the rhythm of the accompanying drums and gongs), became extremely popular.

Her unique blend of dances was named *kabuki odori*. Eventually, the word *kabuki* was written using the previously mentioned characters.

Q As you mentioned earlier, in kabuki the female parts are performed by men, but since when did it become an all-male theater?

What happened was that Okuni began to do her dances dressed up as a man—in fact, like the shocking *kabukimono*. She would depict a male customer flirting the night away with the *chayaonna*, the prostitutes from the brothels. There is a reference

名は慶長8(1603)年の文献に登場します。

　阿国の「かぶき踊り」は大流行し、遊女たちまでが真似をするようになり、「遊女歌舞伎」が発生しました。「遊女歌舞伎」では、遊女が出演し客を取る行為もあったため、徳川幕府は風紀を乱すとして寛永6(1629)年に禁止令を出しました。

　代わって登場したのが、美少年が中心となって演ずる「若衆歌舞伎」です。ところが、この若衆歌舞伎も男色の対象となったため、承応元(1652)年に禁止されました。その後に登場したのが大人の男性のみが演じる「野郎歌舞伎」で、これが今日の歌舞伎の源流となるものです。

　幕府は若衆歌舞伎のシンボルでもあった前髪を剃り落とすこと、歌や舞いよりも芝居を主体にすることなどを興行の条件として出しました。以降、歌舞伎は筋のある写実芸としての発展を遂げることになります。

　また、女性が舞台に立つのを禁じられたことで、男性が女性に扮する歌舞伎独特の「女方」の芸が生まれました。この「女方」は歌舞伎の大きな魅力の1つとなっています。

　政府の弾圧までもエネルギーに転嫁してしまうところに、歌舞伎の俳優と興行者のしたたかさ、その情熱がうかがえます。

to Okuni's *kabuki odori* in documents from Keichō 8 (1603).

Okuni's *kabuki odori* became a big hit, and even the prostitutes started to imitate it, giving rise to the "prostitute kabuki." True to the name, the dancers also sold their favors to the customers. This led to a crackdown by the Tokugawa shogunate, who declared that public morals were being destroyed and decreed in Kan'ei 6 (1629) an official ban on the theatrical appearance of women.

The women were promptly replaced by beautiful young boys in similar dance-drama performances called *wakashu* kabuki. But these adolescent actors in turn began to attract the undue attention of male admirers, and they, too, were banned in Shōō 1 (1652). They were then replaced by mature men in *yarō* kabuki, and this became the forerunner of modern kabuki.

The authorities granted these men permission to perform, but only if certain basic reforms were made. The first condition was that the entertainers would shave their forelocks, which had become somewhat of a symbol of *wakashu* kabuki. Secondly, these shows were to have a stronger story content and emphasize acting over singing and dancing. In effect, what these regulations did was to help kabuki evolve into a dramatic art form.

In addition, the prohibition against women performers gave birth to the role of the *onnagata*, where men dress up as women and play their parts. This *onnagata* has become the cornerstone and one of the principal attractions of kabuki.

We can sense the passion that these actors and others involved in kabuki must have felt for the art, in that they not only persevered, but turned the very forces of governmental repression into a catalyst for transformation.

歌舞伎の発展と出し物の様々

 歌舞伎はその後、どのように発展してきましたか。

A 元禄時代（1688–1704）ごろに、歌舞伎は江戸、上方（大坂、京都）で大きな発展を遂げました。江戸は幕府の置かれた武家中心の新興都市、上方は古い歴史を持つ商人の町でした。人々の趣味嗜好も異なり、江戸では勇壮な「荒事」、上方では優しくなごやかな「和事」と呼ばれる芸が喜ばれました。

荒事とは初代市川団十郎（1660–1704）が始めた芸です。荒々しく豪快で様式的な演技を特色とします。初代団十郎は延宝元（1673）年に14歳の若さで、中村座の芝居「四天王稚立」で坂田公時を演じ、初めて荒事を見せたと言われます。

全身を赤く塗り、顔に派手な隈取りを施して立ち回りを力強く演じ、一躍人気者となりました。荒事の主人公は、人間を超越した力を舞台上で発揮します。荒事は市川家の芸として伝承されました。

和事は荒事とは対照的に、上方の町人社会の嗜好を反映し、優雅で繊細なものとなりま

THE DEVELOPMENT OF KABUKI AND THE VARIETY OF PLAYS

Q How did kabuki continue its development?

Around the Genroku period (1688–1704), kabuki underwent a tremendous evolution in areas like Edo and Kamigata (Ōsaka, Kyōto). Edo was a booming city centered around the warrior class, while Kamigata was a merchant's town with a long history. People's tastes were different too; in Edo, they preferred the more heroic *aragoto* (exaggerated performance), while in Kamigata they preferred the softer and more realistic *wagoto* style.

Aragoto was a style of acting started by Ichikawa Danjūrō I (1660–1704). It was a bombastic, exaggerated style of acting characterized by larger-than-life action. At the tender age of fourteen, in Enpo 1 (1673), Danjūrō I played the part of Sakata no Kintoki in the play *Shitennō Osanadachi* for the Nakamura-za theater, and it is said that that was the first performance of the *aragoto* show.

Danjūrō leaped into popularity with his first rendition of the *aragoto* style of acting. Boldly painting his entire body red, and streaking his face with a vivid, mask-like makeup called *kumadori*, he performed a vigorous *tachimawari* (stylized fighting) on stage. Generally, the protagonist of *aragoto* plays exhibits superhuman strength on stage. *Aragoto* plays have been transmitted from generation to generation through the Ichikawa acting-family dynasty.

In contrast to *aragoto*, the *wagoto* style reflected the elegant and refined tastes of the Kamigata townspeople. The first

坂田藤十郎

した。最初に始めたのは初代坂田藤十郎（1647–1709）です。遊女に恋をして親から勘当を受けた商家の若旦那などを主人公に、お家騒動を描くなど、恋する男性の姿をおかしみを持って写実的に見せました。和事の主人公は荒事と違い、あくまでも優しく、柔らかく行動するのに特色があります。

藤十郎は劇作家の近松門左衛門（1653–1724）と組み、和事芸を完成させました。藤十郎に当てて書かれた近松作品には「傾城壬生大念仏」などがあります。

Q 歌舞伎には、ほかにはどんな種類の芝居がありますか。

竹田出雲

A 義太夫節による人形浄瑠璃が享保時代（1716–36）ごろから上方で人気を博すようになりました。近松、竹田出雲らの作家が優れた作品を発表し、歌舞伎をしのぐ勢いを持ちました。人形浄瑠璃は歌舞伎のように俳優に合わせて作る必要がなく、ストーリーを重要視したため、歌舞伎作品よりも演劇的に見て完成度の高いものも多く生まれました。

そこで、興行側も浄瑠璃の人気に目を付け、作品の歌舞伎化を開始しました。浄瑠璃から歌舞伎に入った作品を、現在では「丸本歌舞伎」と呼びます。

「丸本歌舞伎」は歌舞伎の財産となっていて、人気演目の多くがこの丸本物です。代表的なものとしては、「仮名手本忠臣蔵」（話の概要は58ページ参照）、「菅原伝授手習鑑」、「義経

person to perform it was Sakata Tōjūrō I (1647–1709). He portrayed romantic male leads with realism and a little touch of humor. A typical play would depict some type of family strife; the protagonist might fall in love with a prostitute and be disowned by his parents. In contrast to *aragoto*, the protagonist of *wagoto* typically behaves with civility and gentleness.

Tōjūrō paired up with playwright Chikamatsu Monzaemon (1653–1724) to perfect the *wagoto* style of acting. Chikamatsu's works written for Tōjūrō include *Keisei Mibuno Dainenbutsu*.

What other types of plays are there in kabuki?

Jōruri (narratives recited during bunraku puppet plays) by *Gidayūbushi* became extremely popular in Kamigata during the Kyōho era (1716–36). Writers like Chikamatsu, Takeda Izumo and others came out with these outstanding ballad-dramas that eclipsed those of kabuki. Without the need to take actors into consideration, writers for the *jōruri* could concentrate on the narrative structure, which generally is more logical and more complete than kabuki plays, from the standpoint of drama.

Faced with the popularity of *jōruri*, kabuki adopted certain elements from the puppet plays, including its more intricate plots. Works that have come from *jōruri* are called *maruhon* kabuki.

The *maruhon* kabuki is considered to be an important source of revenue for kabuki. Many popular plays fall under this heading. There are three major representative works called *Kanadehon Chūshingura* (for story summary, see page 59),

千本桜」があげられます。

　丸本物の影響を受け、歌舞伎のために作られた多くの作品には、竹本と呼ばれる太夫による義太夫節と三味線の伴奏が入るようになりました。

 勇ましい武士が、大きな身振りで難しい言葉を使い、
活躍する作品を見たことがありますが、
あれはどんな芝居なのでしょう。

　A それは「時代物」といって、武家社会を題材にした作品のことです。現代の感覚で言うなら「時代劇」です。もちろん江戸時代の人から見た「時代劇」ですから、扱っている年代はそれ以前になります。源氏と平家の合戦や、大名の伊達家に起こった「伊達騒動」などのお家騒動、「忠臣蔵」に代表される仇討ちなどが題材となります。

　衣装は江戸時代の物をベースに考案してあり、演技は様式的であることが特色です。言葉は当時の武家言葉が元になっているので、現代語とはだいぶん異なります。最初は分かりにくいでしょうが、耳になじんでくると聞き取れるものです。

Sugawara Denju Tenarai Kagami, and *Yoshitsune Senbon Zakura* (The Thousand Cherry Trees of Yoshitsune).

Many works influenced by the *maruhon* and created for kabuki started introducing *gidayū* (ballad-drama music). This was created by the chief actor, called *takemoto*, and accompanied by the *shamisen*, a three-stringed lute.

 I've seen plays where courageous warriors use exaggerated gestures and difficult language. What sort of plays are those?

Those are called *jidaimono* (historical piece) and are works whose themes center around the samurai society. They would be the equivalent of what we call *jidaigeki* (historical drama) today. Of course, these are historical pieces from the viewpoint of people in the Edo period, so they are set in an even earlier time period. Their themes include battles between the Genji and Heike clans and the squabbles of the famous Date family or the Daimyō (feudal lords), as well as plays of revenge, as represented by the famous *Chūshingura* (*The Revenge of the Forty-Seven Samurai*).

These plays are characterized by a formalized style of acting, and the costumes are portrayed realistically, after the prevailing fashions of society during the Edo period. The language is quite different than modern spoken Japanese, as it is based on samurai speech of those days. It may be difficult to comprehend at first, but as your ears get used to it, you'll be able to pick out what they are saying.

時代物の後に見た芝居は、もっと分かりやすい言葉を使っていて、今の時代劇のようでした。あれは何と言う芝居ですか。

A 庶民の日常生活や事件に題材を取った作品を世話物と言います。「世間の話題」から「世話」と名が付いたと言われています。

主人公は商人や農民、変わったところでは泥棒などです。江戸時代の庶民の言葉を使うので、現代語とたいへん似通っています。初めて見る人でも楽しめるはずです。世話物は写実的な演技方法をするのが一般的です。

世話物の中でも特に写実的な作品を「生世話」といいます。「生」とは「生一本」などの「生」。純粋で交じりっ気のないという意味です。殺人事件や心中、放火、強盗など世の中を騒がせる事件が起こると、作者たちは素早くそれを題材にした作品を書きました。

Q 歌舞伎の脚本を狂言というようですが、「能狂言」とは違うのですか。

A 歌舞伎は初期のころに「能狂言」からいろいろな素材を取り込みました。また狂言師の中には歌舞伎の成立に参加した者もいました。そのため、歌舞伎の脚本を狂言と言うようになったと考えられています。脚本家を「狂言作者」といいます。

しかし、江戸時代と現代とでは狂言作者の

After the *jidaimono*, they showed a play that used much more easily understood language, much like today's *jidaigeki*. What kind of play is that?

These other plays are called *sewamono*, a genre of plays dealing with the everyday life of common people with its trials and tribulations. It is said that the word is made up of the combination of *seken no wadai* (life topics), which was then abbreviated to *sewa*.

The protagonists are generally merchants and farmers, while the more unusual ones may be thieves. Since the actors use the language of the commoners of the Edo period, they are quite similar to modern Japanese. Even people seeing these plays for the first time should be able to enjoy them. Generally, the *sewamono* employ realistic acting.

Within the *sewamono*, works that are particularly realistic are called *kizewa*. *Ki* stands for the *ki* in *ki ippon*, as in "straight, undiluted, pure." That means they are plain and pure, without affectation. When there was a real-life murder, lovers' suicide, arson, robbery, or other crimes that engaged people's attention, writers promptly created works that used these events as themes.

Q I understand that the script for kabuki is called *kyōgen*, but is that different from nō and kyōgen?

In its early stages, kabuki adopted many elements from nō and kyōgen. Among many kyōgen masters were those who also participated in the creating of kabuki. It's thought that this is why the script for kabuki came to be called kyōgen. The script writer was called kyōgen *sakusha*, or kyōgen writer.

The works of the kyōgen writers from the Edo period,

仕事も大きく異なります。江戸時代には歌舞伎狂言は合作、つまり分業形式がほとんどでした。責任者である立作者（たてさくしゃ）の下に数人の作者が付き、場面ごとに違う作者が筆を取りました。

　明治以降は文明開化の波にのり、合作制度も古臭いものとして否定され、外部の西洋演劇の影響を受けた学者や作家が脚本を書くようになりました。ですから現在では狂言作者が芝居の脚本を書くことはほとんどありません。

　現代の狂言作者は楽屋（がくや）の「狂言部屋」に待機し、黒衣（くろご）を着て俳優のプロンプターをしたり、その俳優の話すセリフのみを毛筆で書き抜いた帳面の「書き抜き」を作ったりしています。歌舞伎俳優は1冊の台本ではなく、自分用の書き抜きでセリフを覚えるのが普通です。

 Q 通し狂言とは何ですか。

　A 最初から最後まで戯曲を省略しない形で上演することを「通し」といいます。江戸時代には朝から晩まで1日がかりでの上演が普通でした。観客はお弁当やお菓子を食べたり、お酒を飲んだりしながら長々と歌舞伎見物を楽しみました。現在は観客も忙しく、自宅も劇場から離れた場所にある場合が多いため、遅くまでの上演はできません。「通し」と言っても、狂言に部分的な省略を加えた上演がほとんどになりました。

however, are very different from what they are today. In the Edo period, most kabuki kyōgen were collaborations, in other words, a team effort. There was the main *tatesakusha*, who was responsible, and under him were a stable of writers. Each scene was written by a different writer.

The period after the Meiji era was one of cultural expansion, and the team-writing method of jointly hammering out a script was rejected as being old fashioned. Influenced by the Western dramatic tradition, scriptwriting became the sole responsibility of scholars and writers. Hence today, there are virtually no scripts created by kyōgen writers.

The modern kyōgen writer waits in the kyōgen room of the *gakuya*, the backstage. Dressed in black, he gives prompts to the actors or creates a *kakinuki* (excerpt) written in ink and brush. This excerpt consists only of the lines spoken by one actor. The kabuki actor normally remembers his lines from this *kakinuki* rather than from the entire script.

Q What is a *tōshi* kyōgen?

Performing a play from start to finish without omitting any acts is called *tōshi*. In the Edo period, it was common to have shows that went all day from morning to dusk. The audience enjoyed these lengthy performances of kabuki by eating *bentō* (box lunch), snacking, or drinking alcohol. But now everyone is busy, and since people's homes are often far from the theater, it would be inconvenient to have the performances running late into the night. Therefore, even if a play is billed as *tōshi*, you are still likely to find some abridgment or omission.

　1つの場面が終わって幕が引かれ、次の幕が開くまでの間を「幕間」または「幕の内」といいます。席や食事の手配は芝居茶屋がするのが普通でした。芝居茶屋では観劇用の弁当を出しました。魚や煮物などいろいろなおかずが入った弁当を「幕の内弁当」といいますが、これは「幕の内」に観客が弁当で食事をしたことの名残です。

　「通し」とは逆に、狂言の中から人気のある場面だけを選んで上演する形式を「見取り」と言います。「見取り」は、好きな物を取ってもいいという意味の「選り取り見取り」の「見取り」から出た言葉だと言われています。例えば「菅原伝授手習鑑」から「寺子屋」の場だけ、「近江源氏先陣館」から「盛綱陣屋」の場だけを上演する場合などがこれに当たります。

Q 得意な物のことを「あれは誰々の十八番だから」という言い方をします。語源は歌舞伎だと聞きますが、どこから出てきた言葉なのでしょう。

七代目 市川団十郎

A 市川団十郎家の代々が得意とした18の芸を集め、七代目団十郎が制定したのが「歌舞伎十八番」です。「十八番」と書いて「おはこ」とも呼びます。

　しかし、その全部が人気があって今でも上演されるかというとそうではありません。例

The interval between the opening and the closing of the scene is called *makuai* or *makunouchi*. The *shibaijaya* (theater tea house) commonly took care of the seating and the meals. These theater tea houses served *bentō* for viewing plays. Today we call a *bentō* with many different dishes, such as fish and *nimono* (simmered foods), *makunouchi bentō*. As you can see, this name was derived from the *bentō* which the audience ate during the *makunouchi*.

In contrast to the *tōshi*, there is another format called *midori*. This is where only the popular scenes from the kyōgen are performed. *Midori* is taken from the phrase *yoridori midori*, which means you can choose the parts you like. For instance, you would see only the *terakoya* (temple school) scene from *Sugawara Denju Tenarai Kagami*, or the *Moritsuna Jinya*, scene from *Ōmigenji Senjin Yakata*.

Q **When we discuss someone's forte, a person's particular specialty, we would say, "That is his *jūhachiban* (number eighteen)." The phrase is supposed to have its etymology in kabuki, but just how did that come about?**

Danjūrō VII compiled an inventory of the most notable plays, acts, and scenes from plays in the repertory of the Ichikawa acting-family dynasty. This is the kabuki *jūhachiban*, or "eighteen kabuki numbers." Actually, it is written as "*jūhachiban*," but read as *ohako*.

This does not mean that all eighteen of the pieces have remained popular today or are still being performed. For

えば「勧進帳」「助六」「暫」などは頻繁に掛かる人気演目です。しかし、「蛇柳」という演目などはすっかり上演がとぎれてしまいました。「鳴神」は、明治以降に二代目市川左団次が復活上演し、再び脚光を浴びることになりました。

助六曲輪菊

歌舞伎の劇場と舞台の様々な工夫

Q 江戸三座という言葉が出ましたが、どんな劇場だったのですか。

A 幕府から興行を正式に許された劇場のことです。興行は許可制で、興行権を持つ者だけが「櫓」をあげて芝居を上演できました。当初は中村座、市村座、森田座、山村座の四座でしたが、山村座が興行権を失ったため三座となりました。

三座は世襲制で、諸般の事情で三座が興行できない場合は、「控え櫓」が代わって興行しました。中村座の控は都座、市村座の控えは桐座、森田座の控は河原崎座でした。

三座の最高責任者を「座元」と言いました。中村座は中村勘三郎、市村座は市村羽左衛門、森田座は森田（守田）勘弥を代々が名乗り、明治時代まで続きました。現在も歌舞伎俳優の

instance, *Kanjinchō*, *Sukeroku* and *Shibaraku* are popular pieces frequently seen today. But plays like *Ja Yanagi* are rarely, if ever, performed. *Narukami* was resurrected by Ichikawa Sadanji II after the Meiji period and has once again entered the spotlight.

KABUKI THEATER AND STAGE MANAGEMENT

 What sort of theaters were the Edo *sanza* (three Edo playhouses)?

These were kabuki playhouses that had official authorization from the shogunate to perform plays. At that time, the entertainment industry was regulated through a permit system, and only those that had obtained the right to produce plays could raise a *yagura* (tower) on the roof of their theater. There were four playhouses in the beginning: the Nakamura-za, Ichimura-za, Morita-za, and Yamamura-za. Later, however, Yamamura-za lost its permit, leaving only three. The operation of these *sanza* were passed down on a hereditary basis.

If, for various reasons, one of the three was unable to stage a production, they would use a reserve, or substitute theater, called *hikaeyagura*, where the performance would be played. Nakamura-za's stand-in playhouse was Miyako-za, Ichimura-za's was Kiri-za, and Morita-za had Kawarazaki-za.

The head managers of the three theaters, called *zamoto*, would assume a special house-identification name for their official capacity. Thus, the head manager for Nakamura-za was called Nakamura Kanzaburō, Ichimura-za's was Ichimura

名前として残っています。

Q 櫓とは何ですか。

A 物見などに使う方形の高い構造物のことですが、江戸時代には興行権のシンボルとして用いられ、三座では劇場正面の屋根の上に設けられました。現在でも、銀座の歌舞伎座や京都の南座には櫓が掲げられています。

幕府から興行を許されず、三座のような櫓を上げられない芝居小屋のことを「小芝居」と言いました。「小芝居」は、江戸時代は寺、神社などの境内や盛り場に作られ、芝居を上演しました。

明治維新後は公的な差別はなくなりましたが「小芝居」の名称は残りました。四代目沢村源之助が活躍した「宮戸座」などが有名です。

Q 芝居の幕が開く時に、
「チョンチョン」と甲高い音が響きました。
あれは何ですか。

A 長方形に削った柝という木片を打ち合わせて音を出しているのです。柝は、拍子木とも言います。狂言作者は、これを打っていろいろなきっかけを知らせるための音を出しま

Uzaemon, and Morita-za's was Morita Kanya. Until the Meiji period, each successive generation of head managers was given these names. Today these same names are assumed by kabuki actors.

 What is a *yagura* (tower)?

Yagura is a tall, rectangular structure which in the Edo period was used to signify that the theater had an official license to perform. The three theaters had *yagura* on top of the roof facing the front entrance. Even today, the tower is raised on top of Tōkyō's Kabuki-za and Kyōto's Minami-za.

Unlike the *sanza*, playhouses that did not have authorization from the shogunate were not allowed to raise the *yagura*. These were called *koshibai*, or small playhouse. In the Edo period, the small playhouses were built within temple and shrine compounds or in amusement quarters where they would stage their plays.

Although this type of distinction was discontinued at the time of the 1868 Imperial Restoration, the name *koshibai* stuck. Among the better known small theaters is Miyato-za, where Sawamura Gennosuke IV performed.

 Just at the point when the curtain is drawn, you hear a high-pitched, clacking sound. What is that?

It's the sound of *ki*, wooden sticks being clapped together. These clappers, also called *hyōshigi*, are a pair of square-shaped sticks made of hard wood. The kyōgen *sakusha*, or stage assistant, uses these clappers as various prompts. The

す。幕を開ける時には、析を小刻みに打ちます。幕切れや、次の幕へ移行するまでの緊張感を持続するためにも析を打ちます。

　舞台の上手の端に、四角い板を置き、「黒衣」を着た係（次の質問参照）がその板を2本の析で叩いて効果音を出すことを「ツケ」と言います。「見得」を切る時や、役者が走る時の足音などにもツケを使います。東京では大道具の係が、関西では狂言方がツケを打つしきたりです。

析とツケ板

Q 舞台の上に、黒い衣装を着た人がいますが、芝居の途中で、何をやっているのでしょうか。

A 歌舞伎の舞台に登場する全身に黒の衣装を着て、黒い頭巾を被った人が「黒衣」です。実際には見えても舞台上の約束事としては見えないことになっている陰の存在です。

　演技の途中で用のなくなった小道具を片付けたり、逆に必要になったものを出したり、俳優を「合引」という椅子のようなものに座らせたりします。雪の場面や水の場面では黒が目立つため、白や青の衣装を付けます。通常は俳優がつとめます。プロンプターは黒衣ではなく狂言方の仕事です。

黒衣

　黒衣と同様に舞台上の俳優を助ける仕事をするのに「後見」がありますが、顔を観客に見せるところが、黒衣との決定的な違いです。素顔で紋付き、袴姿で登場し、舞踊の際の小

後見

sticks are struck together quickly to signal the curtain opening. They are also used to maintain the tension when the curtain closes or the next scene opens.

These wooden clappers are used, as well, for another type of sound effect called the *tsuke*. The stage attendant, who is dressed in black (see below), strikes a square wooden board at stage left with these clappers. The *tsuke* can also be used when the actor is running on stage, or when he assumes a pose called *mie*, which is a set-piece gesture used to emphasize an especially dramatic moment. In Tōkyō, the *tsuke* is struck by an attendant in charge of large props, while in Kansai, the *kyōgen-kata* is in charge.

 What does the person dressed in black do on the stage during the performance?

This figure is the *kurogo*, or "person in black". He appears onstage during a kabuki performance dressed all in black and wearing a black hood. Although he is visible, the theater convention is to disregard him, and hence he remains a shadow figure.

His role is to remove small props that are no longer used, to bring them out when they are needed, or else to make the actors sit in a chairlike piece called an *aibiki*. The *kurogo* may dress in white or blue if there is a snow or water scene where the color black would stand out too much. Normally, the role of *kurogo* is assumed by an actor. The duty of giving prompts is left to the *kyōgengata*, not the *kurogo*.

Like the *kurogo*, there is another assistant, called *kōken*, who helps the actors onstage. The main difference between the two is that the *kōken* shows his face to the audience. He wears no makeup, but appears onstage wearing a crested kimono and

道具の片付けや衣装の着替えの手伝いなどを
します。

　踊り手に舞台上で支障があった場合には後
見がただちに代わるのが決まりです。それだ
けの技量があるものが勤めるとされるのが後
見なのです。「歌舞伎十八番」などでは、市
川団十郎家の紋を入れた柿色の裃を着て、鬘
をつけた姿で登場します。

Q 早替わりとは何ですか。

　A 同じ俳優が1つの芝居で何役かを兼ねて
いるため、素早く扮装を変えることです。人
気俳優の芸の演じ分けや、立役から女方まで
のいろいろな姿を見られるため、観客に喜ば
れます。

　早替わりを売り物にした狂言も多くありま
す。鶴屋南北作の「お染久松色読販」は「お
染の七役」の通称で知られる人気作品です。
この芝居では主演俳優が町娘、田舎娘、二枚
目、悪婆、奥女中、老け役など七種類の役を
替わって見せます。

Q 長い棒の先に鷹が付いたものを
黒衣が操っているのを見たことがあります。
何と呼ぶのでしょうか。

　A これを「差金」といいます。舞台の上で、
竿の先に針金をつけて、これに作り物の蝶や
鳥などをつけて動かすものです。鷹の付いた
差金なら、たぶん「金門五三桐」という芝居

a *hakama* (long, pleated trousers). He cleans up the props used for the dance or helps with the actor's rapid costume changes.

Like an understudy, should anything happen to any of the dancers onstage, the *kōken* is prepared to immediately substitute for the performer. He therefore needs to be a very skilled actor in order to qualify as a *kōken*. In kabuki *jūhachiban*, the *kōken* appears on stage wearing a wig and a persimmon-colored ceremonial dress bearing the family crest of Ichikawa Danjūrō.

Q What exactly is a *hayagawari* (rapid-fire costume change)?

Hayagawari is used when one actor plays many different roles, and therefore needs to change his costume instantaneously. It's a crowd pleaser, as the audience enjoys watching a popular performer showing off his acting skills in many different roles, in guises ranging from a male lead to an *onnagata*.

Many kyōgen plays employ *hayagawari* to attract audiences. The play *Osome Hisamatsu Ukina no Yomiuri*, by Tsuruya Nanboku, is a popular work known commonly as *Osome no Nanayaku* (The Seven Roles of Osome). In this drama, the actor plays seven different roles, including townsmaid, country girl, handsome lover, wicked woman, waiting maid, and an old person.

Q I've seen the *kurogo* wielding a long staff at the end of which a hawk is attached. What is that called?

This staff is called the *sashigane*. A wire is attached to the end of the pole, to which an artificial butterfly or bird is fastened. This is then waved around. If it was a hawk you saw, you were probably watching the scene *Nanzenji Sanmon no*

の「南禅寺山門の場」を御覧になったのでしょう。この場面では大泥棒の石川五右衛門の所に差金に付いた鷹が飛んできます。

舞踊の「鏡獅子」や「保名」では、棒の先に蝶が付いた差金を使いますし、「東海道四谷怪談」では鼠の付いた差金を用います。怪談などで飛ばす人魂も黒衣が先に火を付けた差金を使います。

差金

Q 舞台から客席に向かって出ている道を「花道」と言うそうですが、これはどんな時に使うのでしょうか。

A 歌舞伎専用の劇場では、舞台の下手（客席から向かって左側）から舞台と同じ高さで客席を貫く通路が出ています。これを花道といい、能の舞台と舞台裏を結ぶ「橋掛り」を模倣したものです。当初は斜めに作られていたようですが、現在は直線です。

重要人物の出入りに使用されることが多く、「助六」の助六の出などが有名です。「勧進帳」でも弁慶、義経主従は花道から登場します。花道は舞台の一部でありながら、客席にあるため、観客と役者の距離感を縮め、一体感を増す効果があります。

花道を、上手（客席から向かって右側）にももう1本作ることがあります。2本ある場合下手の花道を本花道、上手を仮花道と呼びます。「御所五郎蔵」のように数人ずつの役者が向

Ba from the play *Kinmon Gosan no Kiri*. In this scene, the hawk attached to the *sashigane* flies toward the grand thief, Ishikawa Goemon.

Buyō dances like *Kagami Jishi* and *Yasuna*, use *sashigane* with butterflies attached to the tip. And in *Tōkaidō Yotsuya Kaidan*, a ghost story, a *sashigane* with a rat appears. In ghost and horror stories, the *kurogo* brandishes a *sashigane* with a fireball at the tip when representing the flying spirit of a dead person.

> **Q** I know that the runway leading out from the stage and towards the audience is called a *hanamichi*, or flower walk, but when is it used?

Playhouses built exclusively for kabuki performances feature a runway built flush with the stage, going from stage left right into the middle of the spectators' seats. This is what is known as *hanamichi*. It is a replica of the passageway that connects the nō stage to the back of the hall. This passageway was slanted at first, but is now level.

Important characters in a play often make their *de* (entrances) and their *hikkomi* (exits) via this runway. A notable example is the entrance of Sukeroku in a play by the same name. In the play *Kanjinchō*, Benkei and his lord Yoshitsune appear through the *hanamichi*. While the *hanamichi* is a part of the stage, because it goes right into the midst of the audience, it serves to reduce the psychological distance between the audience and the actors, creating a bond of sorts.

Sometimes there is another *hanamichi* leading from stage right. When there are two passageways, the one on the left is called *honhanamichi*, and the one on the right is *karihanamichi*, or auxiliary runway. They may be used when several

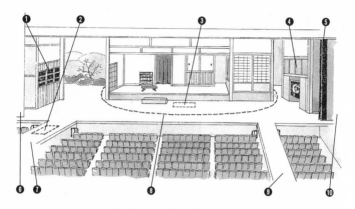

き合って、自分のことを語るセリフを言う場合や、「野崎村」のように、お染と久松が両側に分かれて船と駕籠で引っ込む場面などに使用します。また、花道の間の客席を川に見立て、本花道と仮花道とで言葉を交わしたりすることもあります。

　花道の、舞台から三分、揚幕（花道の出入口に掛けた幕）から七分の位置を「七三」と言います。「七三」の位置で、俳優は見得を切ったり、考える素振りをしたりします。花道での演技のポイントとなる場所です。

　揚幕から俳優が出入りしますが、幕の上には金属でできた輪が付いていて、揚幕が上がって俳優が出る時にはチャリンという音がします。これで俳優の出に観客も気付くという仕組みです。

歌舞伎の舞台

❶ 下座　*Geza* (Box for musicians)

❷ スッポン　*Suppon* (Trapdoor on the hanamichi)

❸ セリ　*Seri* (trapdoor)

❹ チョボ床　*Choboyuka* (Box for the chorus)

❺ 定式幕　*Jōshikimaku* (Draw curtain)

❻ 下手　*Shimote* (Stage right)

❼ 花道　*Hanamichi* (Elevated runway)

❽ 回り舞台　*Mawari butai* (Revolving stage)

❾ 仮花道　*Karihanamichi* (Auxiliary elevated runway)

❿ 上手　*Kamite* (Stage left)

actors face each other to make declamations concerning themselves, as in the play *Gosho no Gorozō*. Or, as in the case of Osome and Hisamatsu in the play *Nozakimura*, there is a parting scene where one person is led away on a boat, while the other goes off on a palanquin. This would be portrayed by having the actors retreat via the two separate runways. Or they might exchange parting words while standing on their respective runways, separated by the audience, which is understood to be the river.

The distance of three-tenths from the stage and seven-tenths from the *agemaku* (stage-entrance) curtain on the runway is called *shichisan*, or seven-three, about seven-tenths of the way down the *hanamichi*. This seven-to-three mark is the point traditionally used for dramatic impact where the actor would strike a *mie* or maybe a pose of deep contemplation.

To make their entrances and their exits, the actors originally had to go through the stage-entrance curtain, on top of which were rings made of metal. The rings would make a sound when an actor pulled up the curtain, thus alerting the audience to his appearance.

Q 舞台の一部が急にせり上がってきておどろきましたが、どんな仕掛けになっているのですか。

A これは「せり」と言って、舞台の下から上へ人や物を昇降させる仕掛けです。建物などの大道具を上へ上げる大せり、人などを上げる小せり、それに「すっぽん」と呼ばれる仕掛けなどの種類があります。

すっぽんは、ちょうど七三のあたりに四角く切った穴です。ここからは魔物などが登場します。「伽羅先代萩」の仁木弾正や舞踊の「将門」の滝夜叉姫の出などが有名です。

Q 舞台がぐるっと回って他の場面が出てきました。これは何という仕掛けなのでしょうか。

A 「回り舞台」と言って円形に切った舞台の床が装置や俳優を上に置いたまま、舞台下の心棒を中心に回転し、代わってほかの装置が登場する機構です。回り舞台があることで、大掛かりな場面転換も一瞬にして可能になります。

歌舞伎の大発明の1つで、宝暦8(1758)年に狂言作家の並木正三が独楽回しにヒントを得て考案したとされます。今では海外でもこの回り舞台が使われています。

以前は人力で回していましたが、現在は電

回り舞台

I was really surprised when a portion of the stage was suddenly raised. How does this device work?

To raise a person or properties from below the stage, a gadget or trapdoor called *seri* is used. There is a big trapdoor for hoisting large structures or equipment, and a smaller one for people, allowing actors to appear or disappear through them. There is also a type of trapdoor called *suppon*, or snapping turtle, so called because of its resemblance to a turtle poking its face in and out of its carapace.

The *suppon* is located at the point of the seven-three on the runway. Ghostly characters appear from this square-shaped opening. Well known are Nikki Danjō of *Meiboku Sendai Hagi* and Nihon Buyō's Takiyasha-hime of *Masakado*.

 The stage made one revolution and a different scene appeared. What sort of mechanism is at work?

The *mawari butai* is a circular platform that can be rotated while a stage set stands on it. It is constructed so that this portion of the stage floor rotates around a shaft below the stage, and then comes up to reveal a totally different scene. Thanks to this *mawari butai*, even large-scale scene changes can be made in a flash.

Mawari butai is one of the greatest inventions of kabuki and is said to have been conceived by Namiki Shōzō, a kyōgen writer in Hōreki 8 (1758), who is said to have gotten the idea from seeing a top spinning. This revolving stage can be seen today in countries outside of Japan.

In the past the stage was rotated manually, but today it is

気仕掛けです。回る円形の床のことをその丸い形状から「盆」といいます。半分だけ回転させ、舞台を一部変化させることを「半回し」、暗い中での回転を「暗転」と言います。

回り舞台ほど大掛かりにはせずに場面の転換を印象づける仕掛けとしては「振り落とし」があります。上から吊ってある水色の幕や黒幕などを一瞬のうちに落とすことです。

代表的な歌舞伎の作品

 Q 「忠臣蔵」とはどんな話なのでしょうか。

忠臣蔵

A 五代将軍徳川綱吉の時代に、今の兵庫県赤穂市にあった赤穂藩の領主である浅野内匠頭が、江戸城内でのいさかいから吉良上野介に切りかかり、取り押さえられて切腹を命じられました。とがめを受けて藩も取り潰しとなり藩士は路頭に迷いました。切り付けられた吉良にはとがめがなかったため、浅野家の家老だった大石内蔵助ら四十七人の家臣たちは、苦労の末に元禄15(1702)年に吉良を自宅に襲い、討ち果たして敵を取りました。

浪士たちは切腹となりましたが、武芸の鍛錬をする者も少なくなった太平の世にあって

operated electrically. Because of the circular shape of the revolving platform, it is called a *bon*, or tray. A half rotation for a partial change of stage is called *hanmawashi*, and a rotation which takes place in the dark is called *anten*.

Another device that can effect a scene change of a smaller scale than the revolving stage is the *furiotoshi*. This consists of simply dropping a pale blue or black screen that is hanging from above.

REPRESENTATIVE KABUKI PLAYS

 What is the *Chūshingura* (The Revenge of the Forty-Seven Samurai) about?

The lord of the *Akō* clan, Asano Takuminokami, lived during the time of the fifth shōgun Tokugawa Tsunayoshi, in what is today the Akō city of Hyōgo Prefecture. One day while inside the castle of Edo, Asano became embroiled in a dispute with Kira Kōzukenosuke and lunged at him with his sword. He was subdued and ordered to commit *seppuku*. Asano's disgrace meant that his clan was destroyed, and its samurai were cast adrift. They became *rōnin* (literally, "wave men"), masterless samurai. But Kira, being the one who was attacked, did not receive an official censure and suffered no losses. Hence, the retainers of the Asano clan, Ōishi Kuranosuke, and the forty-seven samurai plotted revenge. After many years of hardship, in Genroku 15 (1702) they were finally able to attack Kira in his residence and kill him.

Although the forty-seven *rōnin* had to commit *seppuku*, in a peaceful Japan where so few displayed the samurai spirit,

武士の手本と賞賛され、江戸の英雄として親しまれました。現代でも「赤穂四十七士」の名はよく知られ、しばしば映画やテレビなどの題材にもなっています。

芝居の「仮名手本忠臣蔵」はその「赤穂浪士」の討ち入りを基本にして脚色を加えたものです。「菅原伝授手習鑑」、「義経千本桜」と同じく竹田出雲、三好松洛、並木千柳の合作です。人形浄瑠璃用に書かれた作品で、初演は寛延元(1748)年の竹本座です。

赤穂浪士は幕府の処分に背いて仇討ちを行いました。そのため幕府に遠慮して登場人物の名前も本名とは変えてあります。家老の大石内蔵助は大星由良之助、大野九郎兵衛は斧九太夫などとなっています。

Q 「勧進帳」とはどんな芝居ですか。

A 能の「安宅」を基に七代目市川団十郎が初演しました。弁慶、富樫、義経の緊迫したやりとりが見所の上演頻度の高い歌舞伎屈指の人気狂言です。

勧進帳

平家討伐に功績のあった源義経も今は兄の頼朝に追われる身。家来の弁慶たちは山伏に、義経は世話をする強力に姿を変え、富樫が守る関所へと行き掛かりました。

they were hailed as heroes for their show of samurai loyalty, and they became well known figures in Edo. The Akō forty-seven samurai is a household name even today and the subject of numerous movies and television dramas.

The play *Kanadehon Chūshingura* is based on the true story of the Akō vendetta of the forty-seven *rōnin*. Like the plays *Sugawara Denju Tenarai Kagami* and *Yoshitsune Senbon Zakura*, it is a collaborative work by Takeda Izumo, Miyoshi Shōraku, and Namiki Senryō. It was originally created for the *jōruri* puppet theater and was first performed in Kan'en 1 (1748) at the Takemoto-za theater.

Since the Akō *rōnin* disregarded the verdict of the shogunate in carrying out their vendetta, all the names of the characters have been changed out of consideration for the authorities. For instance, the retainer Ōishi Kuranosuke was changed to Ōboshi Yuranosuke, and Ōno Kurobē was changed to Ōno Kudayū.

 ### What sort of a play is *Kanjinchō* (The Subscription List)?

Kanjinchō's first performance based on the nō play *Ataka* was given by Ichikawa Danjūrō VII. It is a popular kyōgen and an outstanding, frequently performed kabuki drama. The play's highlight is the tension-filled exchange involving Benkei, Togashi, and Yoshitsune.

Once a brilliant general who had helped subjugate the Heike, Minamoto no Yoshitsune was reduced to the state of a fugitive fleeing from his elder brother Yoritomo, who sought his life. Benkei and several other of Yoshitsune's retainers disguised themselves as monks, while Yoshitsune pretended to be a porter in their service. Together, they fled towards the

富樫は義経一行が強力姿をしているという
噂があるので通行を許可しません。弁慶はそ
れなら念仏をあげさせてくれと富樫に頼み、
富樫は本当の山伏かどうかを確かめようと質
問をします。

弁慶の見事な返答に感心した富樫は通行を
一旦は許しますが、義経の正体を疑う家来の
声で再び呼び止めます。弁慶は主人ではない
ことを示すために義経を打ち据えます。富樫
は弁慶の忠義に感じ、義経主従と知りつつも
通行を許可するのでした。

Q 曾我兄弟の仇討ちも「忠臣蔵」同様に
歌舞伎で多く上演されるそうですが、
どんな話ですか。

A 源頼朝の治める鎌倉時代に、曾我十郎、
五郎の兄弟が、父の敵の頼朝の重臣、工藤祐
経を18年の辛抱の末に討ち果たしたという
史実が基になっています。能や浄瑠璃、歌舞
伎など、様々な芸能の題材となりました。

江戸三座では正月興行には曾我物を出すの
が決まりで、本来的には関係のない狂言にも
曾我兄弟を登場させたほどです。ことに五郎
は荒事の典型として神格化されました。「歌
舞伎十八番」の「助六」の主人公、花川戸助

barrier-station guarded by Togashi.

Since Togashi had heard the rumor that Yoshitsune and his retinue were disguised as porters and monks, he refuses to give them passage. Benkei then begs to be allowed to recite a sutra, and Togashi asks him questions in an effort to determine whether he truly is a monk.

Benkei gives brilliant answers, and Togashi grants the entourage passageway. They are nevertheless called back by one of Togashi's retainers, who remains suspicious of Yoshitsune's identity. So, in order to prove that the porter is no lord of his, Benkei proceeds to whip him. Although Togashi now realizes that the pair must be none other than lord and vassal, he is so moved by Benkei's display of loyalty, he allows them passage.

 I understand that the Soga Brothers' tale of vengeance is performed as frequently in the kabuki theater as *Chūshingura*. What's the story about?

The tale is based on an actual event that took place during the Kamakura period, in the reign of Minamoto no Yoritomo. The story of the Soga brothers, Jūrō and Gorō, who waited eighteen long years before they could finally avenge the murder of their father by killing his enemy, Kudō Suketsune, the chief retainer of Yoritomo, has been adapted by nō, *jōruri*, kabuki, and other dramatic theater.

It was the custom at the Edo *san-za* to perform a Soga-*mono* play for the New Year's entertainment. Although the story of the Soga brothers did not really belong to kyōgen drama, the brothers would nonetheless make an appearance. In particular, Gorō has become idolized as an archetypal bold,

六も実は曾我五郎という設定です。工藤祐経
に曾我兄弟が対面し、仇討ちの場所への通行
手形を渡される「曾我対面」という芝居もよ
く上演されます。

Q 「東海道四谷怪談」とはどんな芝居ですか。

A 「忠臣蔵」を下敷きにした狂言です。塩
冶家の浪人の民谷伊右衛門はすっかり落ちぶ
れ、今では乳飲み子を抱えた女房のお岩と長
屋住まいをしています。金持ちの伊藤家の娘、
お梅は伊右衛門を好きになり、結婚しようと
思いましたが、それにはお岩が邪魔です。お
梅の乳母は、薬と偽ってお岩に顔の崩れる毒
薬を飲ませます。お岩は真相を知り、恨みな
がら死んでいきます。

伊右衛門はお梅と結婚しますが、お岩の死
霊が取り付き、新婚の晩に誤ってお梅を殺し
てしまいます。実は塩冶家の公金を盗み、犯
行に気付いたお岩の父、四谷左門を殺したの
も伊右衛門でした。お岩の死霊に取り付かれ
た伊右衛門は、狂乱の果てに塩冶浪人でお岩
の義弟になる佐藤与茂七に討たれて死にます。
顔の崩れたお岩が、髪をとかす恐ろしくも
悲しい「髪梳き」は女方芸の見せ所です。ま

東海道四谷怪談

masculine character in *aragoto* (exaggerated performance) plays, which feature courageous heroes. *Sukeroku* is one of the eighteen celebrated kabuki pieces. The play's hero, Hanakawado Sukeroku, was supposed to have been Soga no Gorō. One frequently performed scene is *Soga no Taimen*. This is where the Soga brothers face Kudō Suketsune and receive the passage permit that would enable them to make their way to the spot where they could avenge their father.

Q What sort of a play is *Tōkaidō Yotsuya Kaidan* (Yotsuya Ghost Stories)?

The play is a kyōgen based on the story of the *Chūshingura*. A *rōnin* from the Enya clan, Tamiya Iemon, has fallen in social status. He now lives in a tenement house with his wife, Oiwa, who takes care of their suckling baby. It so happens that Oume, the daughter of the wealthy Itō family, was in love with Iemon and wanted to marry him. But Oiwa was in the way. So Oume's wet nurse gave Oiwa some poison to take in the guise of medicine. This poison would disfigure Oiwa's face when she drank it. Too late, Oiwa discovers the truth and dies with hatred in her heart.

Iemon marries Oume, but Oiwa's vengeful ghost haunts him, causing him to mistakenly kill his bride Oume on their wedding night. As it turns out, Iemon had also murdered Oiwa's father, Yotsuya Samon, who had discovered that Iemon embezzled the Enya clan's government funds. Meanwhile, Iemon is driven half insane by Oiwa's ghost and, in the end, he is felled by Oiwa's brother-in-law Satō Yomoshichi.

Oiwa's horribly disfigured face and the dreadful but tragic *kamisuki* scene where she combs her falling hair are great

た、さまざまな仕掛けも楽しめます。赤ん坊をさらって行く鼠の仕掛け、伊右衛門の抱いている赤ん坊が一瞬にして石の地蔵に変わる仕掛けなどの小さなものから、お岩の死霊が提灯の中から現れる「提灯抜け」という大きなものまでがあります。伊右衛門は悪くて色気のある「色悪」の典型です。

役者の役柄

Q　美男子を「二枚目」といい、語源は歌舞伎だそうですが、どんな役柄なのでしょうか。また男性の役には他にどんな種類がありますか。

立役

A　歌舞伎で男性の役を演じる人を「立役」といいます。二枚目もその1つです。

顔見世の絵看板では、座頭と呼ばれる一座の首席の役者が最初の一枚目に置かれました。次に美男役を演じることの多い人気のある若い俳優の絵が並べられました。つまり、二枚目にならべられたことから、美男子、いい男が「二枚目」と言われるようになったわけです。

「三枚目」とは滑稽な役柄のことで、これも絵看板の三枚目に置かれたことから由来します。歌舞伎に限らず、おもしろい役柄の俳優や、人間関係でそんな役割を演ずる人を三枚目と言います。

showcases for the skills of the *onnagata*. There are also many stage tricks for the audience to enjoy. These range from small ones, like the rat that kidnaps the baby, or the baby that is instantaneously transformed into a stone image of Jizō while Iemon is holding it, to large ones like the *chōchin nuke*, where Oiwa's ghost appears inside a lantern. Iemon, by the way, is the archetype of the unscrupulous rake, the *iroaku*.

THE KABUKI ACTOR'S ROLE

 A handsome man is called a *nimaime*, a word which is said to originate from kabuki. What is the role of this *nimaime*, and what other male roles are there?

Male leads in kabuki are called *tachiyaku*, of which *nimaime* is one category.

When the actors appear at a theater for their premier *kaomise* performance, billboards with their faces drawn are displayed outside. First comes the *zagashira*, the leader of the acting troupe who enjoys star billing. Next to be shown is the popular young actor, who often plays the part of the handsome lover. Since his picture comes second, he is referred to as the *nimaime* or the second one. It was from him that a handsome man came to be called a *nimaime*.

Third in line is the *sanmaime*, meaning third one, again because of the sequence of billboard placement. The *sanmaime* is a comic role, and even outside the sphere of kabuki, actors who play funny roles, or anyone in life who plays the part of a loser is called a *sanmaime*.

　絵看板の順番とは関係ありませんが、現実的な事件に誠実に対処する役を演ずる人を「実役」と言います。「忠臣蔵」の由良之助、「菅原伝授手習鑑」の武部源蔵などがそうです。

　実役と近い役に「捌き役」があります。分別があり、物事を冷静に的確に処理できる信頼のおける男性の役です。「さばいていく」という意味から「捌き役」の名が付きました。「源平布引滝」の実盛、「伽羅先代萩」の細川勝元などがそうです。

　悪人のひどい仕打ちに抵抗せずにじっと耐え忍ぶ役が「辛抱立役」です。「仮名手本忠臣蔵」の「三段目」の高師直にいじめられる塩冶判官、「伊勢音頭恋寝刃」の福岡貢などが典型です。2人とも、こらえにこらえたあげくに怒りを爆発させ、刃を振ることとなります。観客の同情は彼らに集まり、登場人物と一緒に悪人への怒りを募らせるわけです。

 悪人にはどんな役柄がありますか。

　A 立役の中で悪人の役が「敵役」です。敵役にもいろいろな種類があります。天皇の位を奪おうとするような位の高い悪人を「公家

Though this has nothing to do with the sequence in which the picture boards are placed, characters who faithfully render realistic events are called *jitsuyaku*. Examples are Ōboshi Yuranosuke of *Chūshingura*, and Takebe Genzō of *Sugawara Denju Tenarai Kagami*. (The Secrets of Sugawara's Calligraphy.)

Closely related to *jitsuyaku* is the *sabaki* (judgment) role. This is the role of a prudent, trustworthy man who is able to handle matters rationally and appropriately; in other words, a person with good judgment. *Sabaki* comes from the phrase *sabaiteiku* (to judge). Both Tairano Sanemori of *Genpei Nunobiki no Taki*, and Hosokawa Katsumoto of *Meiboku Sendaihagi* are such roles.

Another type of stock character is the long-suffering soul who does not fight back, but continues to endure all the abuse heaped upon him by villains. They are called *shinbō tachiyaku*, or persevering *tachiyaku*. Representative characters are the Enya Hangan, who is bullied by Kōno Moronao, playing the *sandanme* in *Kanadehon Chūshingura*, and Fukuoka Mitsugi in *Iseondo Koi no Netaba*. Both of these characters display patient endurance until finally, unable to contain their pent-up anger, they pull out their swords and brandish them about in an explosion of rage. They have the full sympathy of the audience, who identify with them and feel their own anger building up as they watch these hapless figures being mistreated.

Q **What types of dramatic roles are there for villains?**

The leading villainous role is the enemy, *katakiyaku*. The enemy can also be subdivided into various types, such as the *kugeaku*, the truly heinous villain who attempts to usurp the

悪人（色悪）

悪」、天下国家の転覆を狙う悪人を「国崩し」と言います。

　悪人の中でも、終始一貫して悪の気持ちに徹底した人を「実悪」と言います。歌舞伎の芝居の上では、主君への謀反を企てる明智光秀をモデルにした「絵本太功記」の武智光秀がその例です。また、いい男でありながら、女をだましたりする悪人を「色悪」と言います。「東海道四谷怪談」の民谷伊右衛門がその例です。

Q 顔を白く塗った、なよなよした男の人が舞台に出てきました。あれはどんな役ですか。

つっころばし

　A これを「つっころばし」と言います。上方の和事によく登場する世間知らずの弱々しい色男のことです。悪人に簡単にだまされて周囲に厄介をかける、人騒がせな人物です。忠義な家来や、過去につっころばしの親などに恩を受けたことのある周囲の人間に危難を救われる場合が多いようです。

　同じような優しい見掛けでも「つっころばし」よりは、内面に強さを持つ二枚目を「ぴんとこな」と呼びます。上方の芝居に出てくることが多いようです。「伊勢音頭恋寝刃」という芝居の福岡貢もこの「ぴんとこな」に分類されます。

emperor's throne, or the *kunikuzushi*, one who seeks to overthrow the nation.

The *jitsuaku* is the person who is evil in every fiber of his being. A prototype is Takechi Mitsuhide of *Ehon Taikōki*, who was modeled after Akechi Mitsuhide, the villain who planned an insurrection against his lord. And then there is the handsome but unscrupulous rake who deceives women, the *iroaku*. An example is Tamiya Iemon of *Tōkaidō Yotsuya Kaidan*.

Q **I saw a man on stage who had his face painted white and acted in an effeminate manner. What kind of role is that?**

The *tsukkorobashi* is a character type who frequently appears in the more realistic *wagoto* plays in the Kamigata area. The *tsukkorobashi* is a handsome but weak man who is quite naive about the ways of the world. As a consequence, he is easily tricked by evildoers and creates havoc for people around him who must rescue him from whatever crisis he finds himself in. The rescuers are generally faithful vassals or people who owe his parents a favor.

There is yet another *nimaime* role who may on the surface appear similar to the *tsukkorobashi*, but who possesses a far greater inner strength. This role is called the *pintokona*, and is often seen in plays performed in the Kamigata area. Fukuoka Mitsugi in *Iseondo Koi no Netaba*, would fit this type.

Q 女性の役を演じる女形にはどんな役がありますか。

A 「町娘」「田舎娘」といった娘の役、お姫様の役の「赤姫」、悪事を働くちょっとすごみのある色っぽい女性の役の「悪婆」、一般庶民の家庭の女房役の「世話女房」、御殿などに勤める女性の「片はずし」、格の高い遊女の「傾城」などがあります。

「赤姫」とは変わった呼び方ですが、お姫様役は赤地に色糸で刺繍を施した豪華な衣装を着ることが多いので、この名が付きました。赤と言っても、実際には桃色のこともあります。多くは「吹輪」という真ん中に飾りの輪のはまった鬘を被り、大きな銀の簪を付けます。衣装は袖の長い振袖で、帯は後ろに大きく垂れた振り下げ帯を締めるのが決まりです。

「赤姫」のうちでも特に大役の3役を「三姫」といいます。「本朝廿四孝」の八重垣姫、「鎌倉三代記」の時姫、「祇園祭礼信仰記」の雪姫がそうです。お姫様役の中でも難しく、見せ場が多い役で、多くの女形が目標とする役です。

赤姫

町娘

田舎娘

Q In terms of female characters, what kinds of *onnagata* roles are there?

Young girls' roles include the town girl and the country girl. Then there is the *akahime*, the princess, and the evil woman, the cunningly vicious but seductive *akuba*. There's also the *sewanyōbō*, the devoted wife of a commoner. A woman of rank who works in the palace is the *katahazushi*, and the *keisei* is a high-level courtesan.

Akahime, or red princess, might sound like an unusual name, but it is derived from the gorgeous embroidered red kimono worn for the princess's role. Although the kimono is considered to be red in color, at times it may be closer to a shade of pink. Many of the princess characters also wear wigs called *fukiwa*, which have an ornamental ring fitted into the center, and a large silver hair pin called *kanzashi*. The princess's kimono has long, billowing sleeves, and its *obi* (a sash), is tied so that the sleeves stream down the back.

The *akahime* can be further subdivided into three major types, known as *sanhime*, or three princesses. They are the Yaegaki-hime in *Honchō Nijūshikō*, Toki-hime in *Kamakura Sandaiki*, and Yuki-hime in *Gion Sairei Shinkōki*. Many *onnagata* aspire to play these roles, as they are the most challenging of the princess parts, with so many high points and climactic scenes.

世話女房

悪婆

傾城

舞台化粧と衣装

 役者がいろいろな化粧をしていますが、
化粧によって役柄が異なるのですか。

A 歌舞伎の化粧は役柄と密接に結び付いて
います。顔を赤く塗った人物は敵役で、これ
を「赤っ面」と呼びます。顔を白く塗った人
物は「白塗り」と言って二枚目の役です。

ただし「実悪」(「悪人にはどんな役柄があ
りますか」を参照)の場合は悪人でも顔は赤
く塗らずに「白塗り」で演じます。それによ
って、役柄の冷徹さを一層印象づける効果を
持たせるためです。

女性の役の化粧で特徴的なことの1つは眉
毛で、江戸時代には既婚女性は眉を剃る習慣
だったため、歌舞伎の女方も女房役では眉を
描きません。色気を出すために目尻、目頭に
は紅をちょっとさします。

 顔に筋を描いた人が花道から出てきました。
とても強そうですが、この化粧はどんな意味を
持っていますか。

A 「隈取り」と言って、紅や青などで顔
に筋を描きます。これは血管や筋肉の動きを

STAGE MAKEUP AND COSTUME

 The actors seem to wear so many varieties of makeup. Does the makeup differ depending on the role they're playing?

Yes, kabuki makeup is intimately connected to the nature of the role the actor is playing. Characters with their faces colored red are portraying the enemy, and are called *akattsura*, or red face. Those with their faces painted white are called *shironuri*, or white paint, and they play the *nimaime* role, the handsome beau.

The evildoer classified as a *jitsuaku*, however (see p.69), will have his face painted white, not red. The purpose is to impress upon the audience the character's cool composure.

Eyebrows are one of the unique aspects of women's makeup. It was the custom in the Edo period for married women to shave their brows, so actors playing married women's parts would leave off drawing their brows. But to add a little erotic appeal, they would dab a touch of rouge to the inner and outer corners of the eyes.

Q An actor appeared on the runway wearing makeup in bold colored streaks.
He looks tough, but what sort of significance does the makeup have?

The *kumadori* is an established masklike makeup style where the face is streaked in pigments of red and blue. It is

土蜘蛛隈

公卿悪

誇張したものと考えられます。隈取りは最初は荒事で行われ、やがては広く時代物の化粧として用いられるようになりました。

役柄によって描き方や色が異なります。「暫」や「矢の根」など荒事に登場する力溢れる豪傑は、主に紅で筋を描き、「船弁慶」の平知盛などの亡霊は青い色で、「土蜘蛛」の蜘蛛の妖怪などは、茶を主体にした隈を取ります。

Q 髪にもいろいろな種類があるようですが、化粧と同様に役柄の性格によって変わるのですか。

片はずし

吹輪

伊達兵庫

A 髪も役柄を象徴する場合が多いのです。「片はずし」というスタイルは、髪を輪に結び、こうがい(髪をかき上げるのに用いる細長いもの；簪に似ている)を横に貫き、一方を外した髪形で、「伽羅先代萩」の政岡など、格の高い奥女中がする髪形のことですが、こうした役柄全般を指す呼称としても用いられます。

女方では、お姫様は大きな輪をはめる「吹輪」、「助六」の揚巻などの傾城(遊女)は、髪を頭の頂上に高く結い上げる「伊達兵庫」という鬘を被ります。また、御殿女中などの役は、高島田という鬘を被ります。

立役では、国の転覆などをはかる悪人がする鬘として、頭上高く髪の毛の盛り上がった「王子」、石川五右衛門に代表される大盗賊などの、前額部の髪が伸びほうだいで、上に逆立った「百日」と呼ばれる鬘があります。ま

believed to be an exaggerated depiction of the way the facial blood vessels and the muscles move. *Kumadori* first appeared in an *aragoto* play and eventually came to be used as makeup in *jidaimono*, or historical pieces.

The makeup style and color vary with the role. Larger-than-life heroes brimming with energy in *aragoto* plays such as *Shibaraku* and *Ya No Ne* wear mainly red *kumadori*. By contrast, apparitions like Taira no Tomomori in *Funabenkei* wear blue *kumadori*, while the spider demons appearing in *Tsuchigumo* wear mostly brown *kumadori*.

Q **It seems that there are various wig types. Are they also connected to character, role and type?**

Yes, wigs are very often symbolic of certain roles. There is a style known as *katahazushi*, worn by women of high rank who work in palaces. An example of this is Masaoka of *Meiboku Sendaihagi*. The hair is tied in loops, and a long, thin ornamental hairpin called a *kōgai* is slipped in sideways. You could say that in general the wig connotes this character type.

As for the *onnagata*, princesses wear wigs called *fukiwa*, to which a large ring is attached. Prostitutes in *Sukeroku* wear wigs called *datehyōgo*, where the hair is piled up high. Palace maidservants don wigs called *takashimada*.

Wigs for leading roles include the *ōji*, in which the hair is heaped up on top of the head. This is worn by villains plotting to overthrow the nation. The role of the grand thief, as represented by Ishikawa *Goemon*, also has a special wig called *hyakunichi*. Here, the hair in front is allowed to grow out and

た、分別があり、理非をただす役である「捌き役」の鬘として、油で棒状に髪を固めた「生締（なまじめ）」などがあります。

Q 歌舞伎の衣装には、派手なものや地味なものいろいろありますが、役によってなにか決まりがあるのですか。

A 時代物の武家は豪華な織物の袴、武家の女房は無地の紋付きに打ち掛け姿が一般的です。

「石持（こくもち）」とは紋付きの紋の部分を白い丸に染め抜いた衣装ですが、浪人者の女房の役などにも用います。「菅原伝授手習鑑」の「寺子屋」の戸浪、「傾城反魂香（けいせいはんごんこう）」のお徳などがそうです。「石持」はそんな女房役の代名詞にもなっています。

石持

珍しいところでは近松門左衛門作の「廓文章（くるわぶんしょう）」で、落ちぶれた若旦那の伊左衛門が着る「紙衣（かみこ）」があります。金がないのでいらない手紙を張り合わせて作った服を着るという設定です。実際には紫と黒の配色が美しい着物なのですが、落ちぶれて金のない男の姿も美しく見せてしまう歌舞伎ならではの趣向といえます。

紙衣

主に貧乏な役柄の場合に着るのが「肩入れ（かたいれ）」です。着物の生地が傷んでいることの象徴として肩の部分に違う布が当ててあります。

肩入れ

stand on end. The *sabaki*, or the appraising personality, wears wigs called *namajime*. Here, the hair is stiffened into rodlike shapes using oil.

 Some kabuki costumes are gaudy while others are more subdued. Are there any fixed rules to this?

Generally, samurai in historical dramas wear lavish, embroidered *kamishimo*, while their wives wear *montsuki*, plain crested kimono and an *uchikake*, a long overgarment.

Kokumochi is a *montsuki* where the crests are dyed in white circles. It is worn by the wife of the *rōnin*, the masterless samurai. Tonami, who appears in the *terakoya* Temple School scene in *Sugawara Denju Tenarai Kagami*, and Otoku, of *Keisei Hangonkō*, have become synonyms for such wifely roles.

A rather unusual garment appears in *Kuruwa Bunshō*, written by Chikamatsu Monzaemon. Here, the young master Izaemon, who has fallen in social status, is supposed to be wearing paper clothes made from old letters that he'd glued together. What the audience actually sees on stage is a beautiful kimono in purple and black. But that's how kabuki is: even a character who has fallen upon hard times and is rendered penniless still has to look good.

Kataire is a patch that's sewn on to the shoulders of the kimono worn by impoverished characters. This indicates that the person wearing the kimono is too poor to afford a new one, even though his present garment has become worn out.

役者の演技と見せ場

Q 舞台で俳優が、演技の途中で突然
大きな身振りをしたまま静止しました。
何をしているのですか。

見得

A 役者が感情または動作が最も高揚したときに、一瞬、動きを停止してポーズを作る演技で、これを「見得」と言います。その動作をすることを「見得を切る」と言います。このことから、一般的に、大げさな態度をとることを「大見得を切る」と言うのです。見得を切るときには、「ツケ」という柝を打って、効果音を入れるのが原則です。

いろいろな見得の場面がありますが、「菅原伝授手習鑑」の「車引」で、梅王丸、松王丸、桜丸の三人が絵のように形を決める場面や、「勧進帳」で弁慶が石を投げる形をする「石投げの見得」などがよく知られています。

Q 舞台の上での俳優の動きには、ほかに
どんな特徴のある動きがありますか。

六方

A 右手と右足、左手と左足を一緒に出す動きを「六方」と言います。花道を通って引っ込んで行くときなどでは、スピード感のある六方を見せる場合が多くあり、そこが見せ場となります。「勧進帳」の弁慶の六方などが有名です。

ACTORS' TECHNIQUES AND HIGHLIGHT SCENES

Q During one performance, the actor was right in the middle of a large gesture when he suddenly froze in his movements. What was he doing?

That type of posturing is called a *mie*. When an actor freezes in a dramatic position at the height of an emotion, it is called "striking a *mie*." This is why whenever someone takes an exaggerated attitude, we say that the person is "striking a big *mie*." The theater convention is to have *tsuke* (wooden clappers) struck together to dramatize the effect whenever an actor strikes a *mie*.

There are many scenes in which the *mie* is employed. Some of the best known include *Kurumabiki* in *Sugawra Denju Tenarai Kagami*, where the three characters Umeōmaru, Matsuō-maru, and Sakuramaru perform a simultaneous group *mie* in a pictorial position. The stone-throwing *mie* in *Kanjinchō*, where Benkei poses as if he is lobbing a rock, is another classic.

Q What are some of the characteristic movements of an actor on stage?

Among actors' movements worth mentioning is the *roppō*, (movement in six directions), where the right arm and the right leg, and the left arm and the left leg swing out together. It's often used, accompanied by exaggerated gestures, when an actor makes a dramatic exit via the runway. When the exit is done very fast, as it often is, it becomes the climactic moment of the play. Benkei's *roppō* in *Kanjinchō* is famous.

俳優が人形浄瑠璃の人形を真似て動くのが「人形振り」という動きです。後ろに黒衣が付き、ちょうど人形遣いが人形を扱うように俳優と息を合わせて動きます。俳優はわざとぎくしゃくと動くのがポイントです。「本朝廿四孝」の「奥庭」の八重垣姫や「金閣寺」の雪姫のように感情が高揚した時のほかに、役柄を滑稽に見せようとする場合にも人形振りをすることがあります。

Q 舞台の上で何人もが入り乱れる乱闘シーンには、独特の動きがありますが、どんな約束事になっているのですか。

タテ

A 乱闘シーンを「立ち回り」と言います。現代でも暴れることを「大立ち回りをする」などといい、歌舞伎に語源があります。「タテ」とも言い、俳優が捕り物などの場面で、槍や刀などの道具や素手で争うさまを様式的に見せることです。

トンボ

時代物はゆったりと、世話物はそれよりは少し早い動きで「タテ」がついていることが多いようです。舞踊劇の中での、舞踊化されたリズミカルな立ち回りは「所作立」といいます。「タテ」の時に、主に脇役がする宙返りを「トンボ」といいます。主役が立ち回りで見得を切って見せる際などに、捕り手などが屋根の上などの高い場所から鮮やかに一回転し

Another stylized movement is one that mimics the movements of dolls in the puppet theater, *ningyō jōruri*. This is called *ningyōburi*. Just like a puppeteer manipulating the puppet, a person robed in black stands behind the actor, matching his own movements with that of the actor. The actor deliberately moves in the stiff, awkward manner of a puppet. The *ningyōburi* is used in emotional climaxes, as portrayed by Yaegaki-hime in the scene *Okuniwa*, in *Honchō Nijūshikō*, and by Yuki-hime in *Kinkaku-ji*, as well. It can also be used to make a character appear comical.

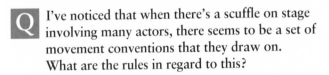

Q **I've noticed that when there's a scuffle on stage involving many actors, there seems to be a set of movement conventions that they draw on. What are the rules in regard to this?**

We call scuffles *tachimawari*. Even today, whenever there's some sort of a skirmish, we call it *ōtachimawari*, or large *tachimawari*, an expression that originates from kabuki. Another term for *tachimawari* is *tate*, a form of stylized fighting. For instance, using stylized gestures and movements, an actor might mime the struggle he undergoes while capturing prey with a spear, a sword, or with his bare hands.

You can observe this *tate* being performed in a slow, leisurely manner in the *jidaimono*, and slightly faster in the *sewamono*. A rhythmic, dancelike *tachimawari* in a dance drama is called *shosadate*.

There is a somersault called *tombo*, or dragonfly, performed mostly by one of the supporting actors during a *tate*. While the hero strikes a *mie* during a *tachimawari*, one of his would-be captors turns a brilliant somersault from a considerable height,

て地上に下り立ちます。

「タテ」の動きの1つに「だんまり」があります。舞台を真っ暗であると仮定して数人の男女が手探りでゆったりと動き、様々な仕種を見せることです。顔見世狂言では必ず「だんまり」を入れる決まりがありました。ストーリー性はほとんどありません。

「タテ」の手順を付ける人を「立師（たてし）」と言います。

Q 滝壺の中での立ち回りで、本当の水を使って俳優がびしょびしょになっていました。あれはどんな演出方法なのでしょうか。

A 歌舞伎の演出の中には、見た目の奇抜さをねらった演出がありますが、これを「ケレン」と言っています。このような、実際の水を使った演出もそうですし、「早替わり」もケレンのうちです。

「つづら抜け」という、衣服などを入れるつづらに入って、手品のように抜け出す仕掛けや、部屋と部屋との間の欄間をくぐり抜ける仕掛けなどもそうです。このような奇抜な仕掛けは邪道と考えられていた時期もありましたが、歌舞伎の楽しみの1つとして、今では広く受け入れられています。

人気のあるケレンの演出の1つとして「宙乗（ちゅうの）り」があります。俳優の体を宙吊りにし、舞台や花道、客席の上で演技させるもので、江戸時代からある技法ですが、現在はワイヤ

宙乗り

such as a roof, and lands gracefully on the stage floor.

Another form of *tate* is the *danmari*, which is a silent scene without any dialogue. The action is supposedly taking place in total darkness. Several men and women on stage grope their way around, moving slowly. The rule is to always include a *danmari* scene during a *kaomise*. The *danmari* has little, if any, plot. It's mostly just action.

The person who creates the choreography for a *tate* is called *tateshi*.

 In one *tachimawari* I saw, the actors actually got drenched in a pool of what turned out to be real water below a waterfall. How did they manage to do that?

Kabuki performances sometimes offer extravagant spectacles for visual appeal. A show using real water is called *keren*. The *hayagawari*, rapid-fire costume change, is also classified as a *keren*.

There's also a trick called *tsuzura nuke*, in which an actor enters and emerges from a box used for storing clothes. An actor proceeding through the transom between rooms is another, similar trick. These stage tricks used to be looked down upon as not being worthy of true drama, but now it is widely accepted as one of the enjoyable features of kabuki.

One very popular type of *keren* is *chūnori*, a midair stunt where an actor is suspended in the air and gives his performance while hovering above the stage, the runway, or the audience. This stage effect has been employed since the Edo

ーロープで吊ることが多いようです。石川五右衛門のつづらを背負っての宙乗りなどが知られます。現代では三代目市川猿之助が得意としています。

　夏場になると主演俳優は避暑のために休暇を取りました。そのため出演料の安い若手俳優などが主になっての興行が行われました。江戸時代の劇場にはもちろん冷房などの空調設備はありません。場内の暑さもひとしおで、観客を飽きさせないために怪談や宙乗り、涼しさを演出するために本当に水を使うなどのケレン的な趣向が好まれました。そうした狂言を夏狂言と言います。

Q 雪の中で女性が吊るされている浮世絵を見たことがあります。歌舞伎の一場面だということですが、これはどんな場面なのでしょうか。

　A 「責（せ）め場（ば）」です。美しい女性や善人が悪人にいじめられる場面です。恋人と別れさせようとする場合や、隠し事を白状させようとする時に、責め場となります。

　雪の中での責め場を特に「雪責め」といい、「明烏夢泡雪（あけがらすゆめのあわゆき）」の浦里（うらざと）や中将姫（ちゅうじょうひめ）の雪責めが有名です。傾城（けいせい）の阿古屋（あこや）に、恋人の居場所を白状させるため琴、三味線、胡弓を弾かせて心の乱れを見るという「阿古屋」の「琴責め」もあります。

雪責め

サディスティックな見せ場です。

period. Today, wire ropes are most often used. A well-known scene is Ishikawa Goemon flying through the air bearing a clothing box. Today, this type of midair stunt is the specialty of Ichiwaka Ennosuke III.

In times past, the summer heat would compel many actors to take their vacation then, leaving mostly younger actors, whose fees were much lower, to carry on with the show. Needless to say, since Edo period theaters lacked air conditioning, so it was quite hot inside. To keep the audience from getting bored and restless in the stifling heat, they offered crowd-pleasing feats like midair stunts, horror stories, and, for a real cooling effect, real water. This type of performance was called *natsu* kyōgen, or summer kyōgen.

Q I've seen *ukiyoe* pictures where a woman is left bound and hanging outside in snow. I hear that they're taken from kabuki scenes, but what are they?

The *semeba*, or place of torture, typically shows a beautiful woman or a good person being mistreated by a villain. Villains might torture a woman to make her break up with her lover or to force a secret out of her that the villains are after.

If the attack takes place in snow, it is called *yukizeme*, or snow torture. Some famous scenes with a backdrop of snow include the torture of Urazato in *Akegarasu*, or the torture of the princess Chūjōhime. In *Akegarasu*, there is also *kotozeme* (torture with the lute) in a scene where the courtesan Akoya is trapped into revealing her lover's whereabouts by being forced to play the *koto*, the shamisen, and the fiddle. The torturers would decipher the truth by sensing her agitation as she plays

殺し場

責め場と同様に、残酷な場面までを様式美に変える歌舞伎独特の見せ場に「殺し場」があります。

「伊勢音頭恋寝刃」で福岡貢が、こらえていた怒りを爆発させて血まみれになりながら、名刀で次々と人を殺める場面や、「籠釣瓶花街酔醒(かごつるべさとのえいざめ)」で遊女八ツ橋を恨んだ佐野次郎左衛門が八ツ橋から始まり、次々と人を殺めて行く場面が知られています。

歌舞伎の舞踊

Q 歌舞伎では舞踊が大きな位置を占めていますが、どのように発展してきたのですか。

A 歌舞伎という言葉に「歌」と「舞」という言葉がある通り、歌舞伎が歌と踊りという2つの要素から始まったことは、最初の歌舞伎の起源で説明した通りです。

歌舞伎の舞踊は最初は柔らかく繊細な長唄が主流でした。長唄は、江戸の歌舞伎の舞踊曲として発達した三味線音楽です。初代中村富十郎(1719-86)や初代瀬川菊之丞(1693-1749)などの女方が得意としました。

宝暦時代(1751-64)になって初代中村仲蔵(1736-90)など、立役の名手が出現し、浄瑠璃を使った豪快な踊りが隆盛になりました。

歌舞伎では、舞踊、または舞踊劇など、長

these musical instruments. It is indeed a sadistic climax.

Similar to *semeba* is another climax unique to kabuki, where even a display of utmost cruelty is transformed into one of ritualistic beauty. This is what is known as *koroshiba*, the killing scene. A good example is the scene from *Iseondo Koi no Netaba*, where Fukuoka Mitsugi lets his pent up rage explode. Even as he is splattered with blood, he slashes people to death one after the other with his sword. Another celebrated scene is from *Kagotsurube Satono Eizame*. Out of hatred for the prostitute Yatsuhashi, Sano Jirōzaemon murders her and then continues in his rampage of murder.

KABUKI DANCE

 Q Dance occupies a huge role in kabuki. How did this develop?

As I have explained in the origin of kabuki, the word *kabuki* contains the words for "song" and "dance," these being the first two elements of the word.

The accompaniment for kabuki dance was mainly the refined and gentle *nagauta*. *Nagauta* are songs to accompany dances that are sung to the shamisen of Edo period kabuki. Nakamura Tomijūrō I (1719–1786) and Segawa Kikunojō I (1693–1749), both female-role players, excelled at this.

After the Hōreki era (1751–1764), Nakamura Chūzo I (1736–1790) and other virtuoso leading men came on stage, and a stirring dance using the *jōruri* flourished.

The *shosagoto* is a group of plays in the kabuki repertoire

唄を伴奏とするものを「所作事」と言います。

Q 「変化舞踊」という踊りはどんな踊りですか。

藤娘

A 文化（1804–18）・文政（1818–30）時代に入ってから流行した踊りです。

「変化」は「妖怪変化」から来ています。妖怪は姿をいろいろな物に変えます。それと同じように俳優が扮装を何通りにも変えて踊るのが「変化物」「変化舞踊」です。元禄10（1697）年に女形の初代水木辰之助（1672–1745）が七通りの姿を見せる七変化を踊り話題を呼んだのが始まりとされます。三変化、五変化から十二変化まで、何通りもの踊りがあります。

鷺娘

江戸に三代目坂東三津五郎（1775–1831）、上方に三代目中村歌右衛門（1778–1838）と東西に2人の舞踊の名手が現れ、歌右衛門が江戸に進出したのを契機に、競って新作を生み出すようになりました。

現在ではその作品の全部を通して踊ることはめったになく、一部だけを上演するのが普通です。「藤娘」「鷺娘」「供奴」「三社祭」などの人気演目も、元は変化舞踊の一部でした。

ところで、舞踊の動きを考案することを「振り付け」といい、振り付けをする人のことを「振付師」と言います。

同じ踊りでも振付師によって、役の心理や

that includes *nihon buyō*, as well as dance-drama.

Q What kind of a dance is *henge-buyō* (transformation dance)?

Henge buyō was a dance that became popular after it was introduced in the Bunka (1804–1818) and Bunsei (1818–1830) eras. *Henge* is an abbrevation of the expression *yōkai henge*. *Yōkai* means "demons and goblins," and *henge* means "change." Goblins are believed to be capable of changing their shape into many forms and, therefore, an actor who makes many costume changes while dancing is referred to as a *henge-mono*. The dance is said to have been first introduced in Genroku 10 (1697) when the *onnagata* Mizuki Tatsunosuke I (1673–1745) created a stir by doing a dance in which he changed his appearance seven times. There are different dance forms involving three, five, or twelve transformations.

Two masters of *nihon buyō* emerged in the east and west of Japan. They were Bandō Mitsugorō III (1775–1831), in Edo, and Nakamura Utaemon III (1778–1838), in Kamigata. When Utaemon moved out into Edo, the two virtuoso dancers competed with each other to compose new dance pieces.

It is rare today to see a performance of the entire repertoire, as generally only a few will be selected for any given show. Popular numbers like *Fuji Musume*, *Sagi Musume*, *Tomoyakko* and *Sanja-matsuri* were in the beginning a part of *henge-buyō*.

The art of creating *buyō* dance steps is called *furitsuke*, or choreography, and the person who does this is known as a *furitsuke-shi*, or choreographer.

Even with the same dance piece, depending on the choreog-

表現法、手順が変わってきます。最初は俳優が自分で振り付けをしていましたが、やがて振り付けを専門の仕事とする振り付け師が登場するようになりました。文化・文政期に変化舞踊の振り付けなどに活躍した三代目藤間勘兵衛、明治時代に「船弁慶」や「土蜘蛛」の振り付けをした初代花柳寿輔などが有名です。

 Q 踊りの題に「道行」という言葉が入っていましたが、これは何を意味するのですか。

A 男女がある場所から目的地へ行くまでの道中を舞踊で見せることです。恋する男女の逃避行、心中の場所へと向かう場合が一般的です。しかし、例外もあります。「仮名手本忠臣蔵八段目」の戸無瀬と小浪は母と娘ですし、「義経千本桜」の「吉野山」の狐忠信と静御前は主人と従者、それも狐と人間との道行です。

道行

rapher, the entire routine, including the psychology of the role and the expressive manner, may differ considerably. In the beginning, the dancer himself made up the dance, but eventually a professional choreographer appeared on the scene. Famous choreographers are Fujima Kanbē III, who worked on *hengebuyō* in the Bunka and Bunsei eras, and Hanayagi Jusuke I, from the Meiji era, who did the *furitsuke* for *Tsuchigumo* and *Funa Benkei*.

 One of the titles of the dances contains the word *michiyuki*. What does that refer to?

Michiyuki refers to the path, shown in the dance, through which a couple travels until they reach their destination. Generally, the couple are lovers running away together or traveling toward the place where they are going to commit joint suicide. There are, however, exceptions. In act eight of *Kanadehon Chūshingura*, the pair, Tonase and Konami, are mother and daughter. Kitsune Tadanobu and Shizuka-gozen, in the scene *Yoshino-yama* from *Yoshitsune Senbon Zakura*, are master and servant. In fact, they are a fox and a human traveling together.

歌舞伎の音楽

Q 舞台の後ろの段の上で、唄を歌ったり、
三味線を弾いたりしていますが、
歌舞伎の音楽にはどんな特徴があるのでしょうか。

三味線

A 歌舞伎の舞踊の伴奏音楽として最初に発展したのが「長唄」です。三味線、唄、鳴物で構成されています。後には、長唄の演奏だけが行われるようにもなりました。

歌舞伎の舞台では、正面の「雛段」と言われる高くなった段の上で演奏することもあれば、舞台下手の黒い御簾を掛けた、客席から見えない場所で演奏することもあります。

舞台上での演奏を「出囃子」と言って、演奏者は袴を着用します。

黒い御簾の中で演奏する音楽を「下座音楽」とも言います。これは、歌舞伎のセリフ劇の効果を出す音楽と言えます。演奏で町の中、田舎、あるいは宮殿の中といった情景の描写を助けます。俳優の喜怒哀楽を音楽で助ける場合もあり、BGMと考えればいいでしょう。

下座音楽

演奏するのは長唄の演奏家ですが、下座音楽

KABUKI MUSIC

 I see musicians sitting in the back of the stage singing and playing the shamisen (three-stringed plucked lute). What are some of the characteristics of kabuki music?

The first kabuki music to develop was *nagauta*, which is dance music used as an accompaniment to kabuki dance. It consists of shamisen, singing, and percussions. Later, there were times when the *nagauta* was peformed by itself, not as an accompaniment.

During the kabuki performance, the musicians either perform in front while seated on the step called *hinadan*, or they create offstage music by playing out of sight of the audience, behind a black bamboo screen which is situated on the left side facing the stage.

The visible orchestra is called *debayashi*, and all members of the ensemble are attired in *kamishimo*, a type of ceremonial clothing.

Offstage music behind the black bamboo curtain is referred to as *geza* music. Music is an integral part of the art of kabuki and serves many functions in the overall dramatic impact of this theatrical art form. It accompanies the chanting or the speaking of the actors' lines and can serve as a scene builder for a town, the country, or the palace shown on stage. Music can also dramatize the emotions of joy, anger, and sadness, as portrayed by the actors. And, of course, it can also be simple background music. The ensemble consists of instrumentalists and vocalists of *nagauta*. However, *geza* music, which of course

には、長唄はもちろん、朝廷の儀式などで演奏される雅楽、能楽、浄瑠璃など、さまざまなジャンルの要素が取り込まれています。

 Q やはり歌舞伎の伴奏になる「常磐津」と「清元」はどんな音楽ですか。

A 常磐津は浄瑠璃節の一派である豊後節から分かれて、歌舞伎音楽として発達しました。豊後節は享保時代（1716–36）に生まれたものです。常磐津は、半ば唄い、半ば語るといった感じで演奏され、美しい曲調に特徴があります。三味線には太棹、中棹、細棹の3種類がありますが、中棹を用います。

清元も常磐津と同じく豊後節から分かれました。文化11（1814）年に初代の清元延寿太夫が創始しました。高音の粋で繊細な曲風が特徴で、多く歌舞伎、舞踊に用いられて今日に至っています。三味線はやはり中棹を使います。

代表的な歌舞伎狂言作家

Q 歌舞伎の作者で「鶴屋南北」の名をよく耳にしますが、どんな人だったのですか。

A 鶴屋南北は元は俳優の名前でした。作者として有名な南北（1755–1829）は四代目で、文化・文政期を代表する作者です。町の片隅に住む民衆の描写に優れました。人間の本質

includes *nagauta*, incorporates various genres, such as the music accompanying nō and *jōruri*, and *gagaku*, the ceremonial music played at court rituals.

 What sort of music is *tokiwazu* and *kiyomoto*, which also served as an accompaniment to kabuki?

Tokiwazu developed as kabuki music after spliting off from Bungobushi, which was a school of *jōruri*, the puppet theater. The Bungobushi school was born in the Kyōho era (1716–1736). *Tokiwazu* is half chanted, half spoken, and carries a beautiful tune. There are three different kinds of shamisen: the *futozao*, *chūzao*, and *hosozao*. Of the three, the *tokiwazu* uses the *chūzao*.

Like *tokiwazu*, *kiyomoto* also split from the Bungobushi school, and was created in Bunka 11 (1814) by Kiyomoto Enjudayū I. It is characterized by high-pitched, delicate tunes. It is still used, mostly in kabuki and dance. *Kiyomoto* also uses the *chūzao* for its shamisen.

REPRESENTATIVE KABUKI PLAYWRIGHTS

 Among kabuki playwrights, I often hear the name Tsuruya Nanboku. What sort of a person was he?

Tsuruya Nanboku was originally the name of an actor. The actor who became the illustrious dramatist was Nanboku IV (1755–1829), a playwright who represents the Bunka-Bunsei era. He was especially skilled at portraying the huddled

をえぐり出すような独創的な作品の数々は普遍性を持ち、歌舞伎のみならず、新劇や小劇場などでもしばしば上演されます。

代表作としては、「東海道四谷怪談」「盟三五大切」「時桔梗出世請状」「桜姫東文章」などがあげられます。

Q 河竹黙阿弥も教科書に出てくるような有名な歌舞伎作者ですが、どんな人だったのですか。

河竹黙阿弥

A 黙阿弥(1816–93)は幕末から明治にかけて活躍した歌舞伎最後の大作者です。現役時代は二代目河竹新七を名乗り、引退してから黙阿弥の名になりました。世話物に優れ、泥棒を主人公にした作品が多いことから、泥棒を白浪というのにちなんで「白浪作者」とも言われました。

幕末には名優の四代目市川小団次とコンビを組み、七五調のテンポのいい台詞で傑作を次々と生み出し、小団次没後は五代目尾上菊五郎や九代目市川団十郎、初代市川左団次などに作品を提供しました。

代表作には「白浪五人男」、「天衣紛上野初花」、「髪結新三」、「十六夜清心」、「三人吉三」、「盲長屋梅加賀鳶」などがあります。

「白浪五人男」の正式な題は「青砥稿花紅彩画」ですが、「弁天小僧」の通称でも親しま

masses living in the obscure parts of a town. There is a universality to many of his original works that cuts to the very core of human nature. His works are performed not only in kabuki, but also in new and small-group theaters.

Representative works are *Tōkaido Yotsuya Kaidan*, *Kamikakete Sango Taisetsu*, *Toki mo Kikyō Shusseno Ukejō*, and *Sakura-hime Azuma Bunshō*.

Q **Kawatake Mokuami was also a famous kabuki playwright frequently mentioned in textbooks. What sort of a person was he?**

Mokuami (1816–1893) was kabuki's last major writer who was active from the last days of the Tokugawa shogunate to the Meiji period. While he worked, he called himself Kawatake Shinshichi II and, after his retirement, he took on the name of Mokuami. He had a special flair for *sewamono*. Many of his plays featured the thief as the protagonist, and since thieves are called *shiranami* (white wave), he was at times also known as the *shiranami* writer.

At the end of the Tokugawa era, he teamed up with Ichikawa Kodanji IV. Together, they created masterpiece after masterpiece. Seven-and-five-syllable lines spoken by the actors move the plays at a good tempo. After the death of Kodanji, he offered works to Onoe Kikugorō V, Ichikawa Danjūrō IX, and Ichikawa Sadanji I, among others.

Representative works include *Shiranami Gonin Otoko*, *Kumonimagou Ueno no Hatsuhana*, *Kamiyui Shinza*, *Izayoi Seishin*, *Sannin Kichisa*, and *Mekura Nagaya Umega Kagatobi*.

The official title of *Shiranami Gonin Otoko* is *Aotozōshi Hanano Nishikie*, but it is also known as *Benten Kozō*. The

れています。弁天小僧、南郷力丸、忠信利平、赤星十三郎、日本駄右衛門の5人の盗賊が活躍します。名場面とされるのが「浜松屋」です。

弁天小僧は女装の盗賊です。美しい娘の姿で、仲間の南郷と一緒に呉服店「浜松屋」を訪れ、難癖を付けてゆすりを働きますが、男と見破られます。この時に切る啖呵(だんか)は名台詞として知られています。続いてが「稲瀬川勢揃い」。5人の盗賊が川を背景に美しい着物姿で立ち回りを見せます。弁天小僧の姿は正月の羽子板の図案などとしてもおなじみです。

歌舞伎役者と屋号

 市川団十郎の名はよく耳にしますが、いったいどんな俳優だったのでしょうか。

A 団十郎家は、初代団十郎(1660–1704)以来、名優を輩出した江戸歌舞伎を代表する家柄です。初代は荒事を創始し、七代目(1791–1859)が「歌舞伎十八番」を制定しました。現在の団十郎は十二代目です。

七代目団十郎の子として生まれた九代目団十郎(1838–1903)は、幕末から明治に活躍し、現在の歌舞伎の礎を作ったことで有名です。

play stars five burglars, Benten Kozō, Nangō Rikimaru, Tadanobu Rihei, Akaboshi Jūzaburō, and Nippon Daemon. A famous scene from the play is *Hamamatsu-ya*.

Benten Kozō is a burglar who impersonates a woman. Dressed up as a beautiful young woman, he visits the kimono shop *Hamamatsu-ya* with his partner Nangō. There, he tries to find fault and blackmail the owner, but his disguise is seen through. One very famous kabuki line is the threat he blusters out when his deception is discovered. Next, there is a scene known as *Inasegawa Seizoroi*. Dressed in beautiful kimonos, and against the backdrop of a river, the five burglars engage in *tachimawari*, stylized fighting. The figure of Benten Kozō is a familiar figure on the battledore commonly seen at New Year's.

KABUKI ACTORS AND THE YAGŌ

 I often hear the name of Ichikawa Danjūrō. What sort of an actor was he?

The Danjūrō family dynasty is an acting-family dynasty that is considered representative of Edo kabuki. The family has produced famous actors since the days of Danjūrō I (1660–1704). Danjūrō I created the *aragoto*, and Danjūrō VII assembled the kabuki *jūhachiban*, the celebrated collection of kabuki vignettes. The current Danjūrō is the twelfth.

Danjūrō IX(1838–1903) was born as the son of Danjūrō VII and was active from the last days of the Tokugawa shogunate to the Meiji period. He is credited with laying the foundation of modern-day kabuki.

九代目 市川団十郎「暫」

九代目は控え櫓の河原崎座の座元の養子となりましたが、兄の八代目団十郎が自殺したため、市川家に戻り、明治7(1874)年に九代目団十郎を襲名しました。演技者としてはもちろん舞踊家としても優れ、「劇聖」と呼ばれました。

また、九代目は歌舞伎の改革にも尽力しました。その1つが「活歴物」と呼ばれる史劇を始めたことです。団十郎は作家や学者などと交流を持つうちに、歴史考証を重視しない従来の歌舞伎の作り方に疑問を持つようになりました。

彼は内容や衣装を史実に忠実にし、大げさな身振りは止め、表情などで気持ちを現す「腹芸」と言われる演技形式を取り入れた新作の芝居を次々と上演しました。「酒井の太鼓」「高時」「大森彦七」などの作品がそれです。活歴物を中心に九代目が制定した家の芸は「新歌舞伎十八番」と呼ばれています。

 **明治以降の有名な歌舞伎俳優には
どんな人がいますか。**

A 九代目市川団十郎と共に「団菊左」と言われて明治の演劇界をリードした立役が、五代目尾上菊五郎(1844–1903)と初代市川左団次(1842–1904)です。九代目団十郎の時代物に対し、菊五郎は世話物を得意とし、弁天小

Danjūrō IX became the adopted son of the head manager of the Kawarazaki-za theater, but because his older brother, Danjūrō VIII committed suicide, he returned to the Ichikawa family. As the successor to the family line, he was given the name Danjūrō IX. He excelled not only in acting but also in dance, and was hailed as a *gekisei*, or the Saint of Drama.

He also lent a hand in the transformation of kabuki. One way in which he did this was to start a historical play genre called *katsurekimono*. As Danjūrō began to associate with writers and scholars, he began to feel that kabuki plays did not concern themselves enough with historical research.

As a result, he adhered closely to historical truth in his narrative and was faithful in his rendition of period costumes. Furthermore, he did away with exaggerated, bombastic gestures, replacing them with an acting style called *haragei*, which sought to express emotions through facial expressions. Works in this style include *Sakai no Taiko Takatoki*, and *Ōmori Hikoshichi*. This family art that Danjūrō IX assembled with *katsurekimono* in the center is called *shin kabuki jūhachiban*, or the "new eighteen kabuki numbers."

Q Who are the most famous kabuki actors in and after the Meiji period?

Onoe Kikugorō V (1844–1903) and Ichikawa Sadanji I (1842–1904) were considered the two foremost actors in the leading man's role in the Meiji world of drama. They, together with Ichikawa Danjūrō IX, were called *Dankikusa*. While Danjūrō IX did historical pieces, Kikugorō's specialty was

五代目　尾上菊五郎

五代目　中村歌右衛門

僧、髪結新三などを当たり役としました。

　初代左団次は四代目市川小団次の養子で、立派な容姿と優れたセリフ回しで「丸橋忠弥」など河竹黙阿弥の歴史劇などで活躍しました。

　団菊左没後の歌舞伎界に君臨したのが女形の五代目中村歌右衛門（1865–1940）です。気品と美貌を兼ね備え、「鏡山」の尾上、「伽羅先代萩」の政岡などの古典から、坪内逍遥作「桐一葉」の淀君などの新作歌舞伎までを巧みに演じました。

　その後の演劇界で「菊吉」と言われて人気を博したのが六代目尾上菊五郎（1885–1949）と初代中村吉右衛門（1886–1954）です。六代目菊五郎は五代目菊五郎の子で、父譲りの世話物を得意としたほか、舞踊にも優れた芸を見せました。吉右衛門は義太夫狂言を得意としました。

 Q 歌舞伎俳優は名前以外に屋号と言われるものを持っていますが、どんな由来があるのですか。

　A 江戸時代には武士階級以上でないと名字を使用することができませんでした。歌舞伎俳優の市川、中村などは名字ではなく、あくまでも芸名でした。市川も中村も尾上も歌舞伎俳優にはたくさんいます。そこで区別をするために、歌舞伎俳優は名字替わりに芸系ごとに屋号を持ちました。今でも屋号はその家

sewamono, and his successful roles include Benten Kozō and Kamiyui Shinza.

Sadanji I was the adopted son of Ichikawa Kodanji IV. In addition to his good looks, he was noted for the excellence of his delivery. He was active in historical drama such as *Marubashi Chūya*, written by Kawatake Mokuami.

The actor who reigned in the kabuki world after Dankikusa was the *onnagata* Nakamura Utaemon V (1865–1940). With his grace and beauty, he skillfully played various roles ranging from classics such as Onoe of *Kagamiyama* and Masaoka of *Meiboku Sendai Hagi*, to new plays such as Yodogimi of *Kirihitoha*.

Following Nakamura Utaemon V, the most popular actors were Onoe Kikugorō VI (1885–1949), who was known as "*Kiku Kichi*," and Nakamura Kichiemon I (1886–1954). Kikugorō VI was the son of Kikugorō V and, just like his father, he was accomplished in the *sewamono*. He also displayed his skills in *nihon buyō*. Kichiemon I's forte was *gidayū* kyōgen.

Q **In addition to their regular names, kabuki actors have special house identification names called *yagō*. How did this practice originate?**

In the Edo era, only those who belonged to the class of samurai or above were allowed to have family names. Names such as Ichikawa, and Nakamura, which were attached to kabuki actors, were not family names but strictly stage names. There are many kabuki actors who go by the name of Ichikawa, Nakamura, or Onoe. To distinguish among them, instead of using a family name, they would have *yagō* house identifica-

の象徴として使用されています。

三升

重ね扇に抱き柏

祇園守

丸にいの字

市川団十郎家は成田屋、尾上菊五郎家は音羽屋、中村歌右衛門家は成駒屋、片岡仁左衛門家は松島屋、坂東三津五郎家は大和屋、中村吉右衛門家は播磨屋、松本幸四郎家は高麗屋が屋号です。

歌舞伎の劇場に行くと芝居の盛り上がった箇所や、見得などの俳優の見せ場に、「成田屋」とか「成駒屋」とか、屋号や住まいのある町名を大声で叫ぶ人がいます。この声を「掛け声」といい、声を掛ける人たちを「大向こう」と呼びます。「大向こう」とは劇場後方の立ち見席のこと。そこに同じ芝居を何度も見に通い、声を掛けるような芝居好きが陣取ることが多いため、この名が付きました。

屋号同様に俳優と家を象徴する意味を持つものに「紋」があります。浴衣や手ぬぐい、配り物の扇子などに紋がよく描かれます。市川団十郎家の「三升」、尾上菊五郎家の「重ね扇に抱き柏」、中村歌右衛門家の「祇園守」、沢村宗十郎家の「丸にいの字」などが有名です。

Q 襲名とは何ですか。

A 俳優が今までより大きな名に改名することです。ほとんどの場合は師匠、親、親戚などの所縁の名前を継ぎます。1998年には片岡

tion names, based on which kabuki acting family dynasty they belonged to. Even today, the *yagō* is used as the symbol of a kabuki house.

The Ichikawa Danjūrō lineage had the *yagō* of Naritaya, Onoe Kikugorō had Otowaya, Nakamura Utaemon had Narikomaya, Kataoka Nizaemon had Matsushimaya, Bandō Mitsugorō had Yamatoya, Nakamura Kichiemon had Harimaya, and Matsumoto Kōshirō had Kōraiya.

If you go to a kabuki playhouse, you will hear members of the audience cheer their favorite actors at certain timely moments during a performance, such as when the actor strikes a *mie*. They might yell out the *yagō* Naritaya or Narikomaya, or the name of the town that the actor resides in. This is called *kakegoe*, and these fans are called *ōmukō*, which actually refers to the standing room in the back of the theater. These avid theater lovers, who were given to enthusiastic cheers, would come to see the same play many times installing themselves in the back section of the playhouse.

Like the *yagō*, the *mon*, or family crest, symbolizes the actor's house. The crest is often pictured on bathrobes, towels, and other objects. Famous ones are the *mimasu* of Ichikawa Danjūrō's house, *kasaneōgi ni dakikashiwa* of Onoe Kikugorō's house, *gion mamori* of Nakamura Utaemon's house, and *maru ni i no ji* of Sawamura Sōjūrō's house.

 What is a *shūmei*?

Shūmei refers to the promotion of an actor when he becomes the successor of a given stage name. The actors are most frequently given the names of their teachers, parents, rel-

孝夫が、父が十三代目を名乗った仁左衛門の名を十五代目として襲名しました。団十郎家では海老蔵から団十郎、菊五郎家では菊之助から菊五郎と、たいていは段階を踏んで大きな名を襲名していきます。名前を継ぐことは芸系を継承する意味も持ちます。

襲名の場合は、劇場で襲名披露興行があり、幹部俳優が口上を述べます。口上とは、初舞台や襲名、追善興行などで、俳優が舞台上から観客に挨拶をすることです。芝居の合間に俳優が衣装のまま言うのを「劇中口上」、終演の際に俳優が扮装したままで言うのを「切口上」と言います。口上のために一幕を設ける場合は俳優は家紋を付けた裃姿で舞台に正座して横一列に並び、観客に挨拶をします。

十五代目 片岡仁左衛門を襲名する片岡孝夫

Q **歌舞伎俳優は世襲制ですか。**

A 歌舞伎俳優の子供が俳優になることが多いのは事実ですが、世襲に限定されたわけではありません。血縁者を主体に九代目まで続いた市川団十郎家などは、むしろ例外的な存在です。江戸時代は見所のある弟子を養子にして継承した家がほとんどです。血縁による

atives, and others connected to the theater. In 1998, Kataoka Takao, whose father had been Nizaemon XIII, became Nizaemon XV. The actors are normally promoted to a more illustrious name in a step-by-step process. The Danjūrō family proceeds from Ebizō to Danjūrō, the Kikugorō family goes from Kikunosuke to Kikugorō. To succeed to such a stage name means to inherit the lineage.

The ceremony for receiving the *shūmei* is held at the theater, where the executive actor will give a *kōjō*. *Kōjō* refers to the greetings that an actor makes to the audience on the occasion of his first stage appearance and when receiving a new stage name. *Kōjō* is also given in the performance of Buddhist memorial services. When the actor makes the greeting still in costume between plays, it is called *gekichū kōjō* or between-play *kōjō*. But if the actors give the greeting at the end of the show, while they are still in role, the greeting they give is called *kiri kōjō*, or cutting *kōjō*. If they set up an act for the purpose of giving the *kōjō*, the actor will appear attired in a *kamishimo*, a ceremonial dress, bearing his family crest. He will take his place in line where the actors are queued up, and seating himself in the proper manner on the stage floor will greet the audience.

Does kabuki follow a hereditary system?

While it's true that many children of kabuki actors follow the tradition, kabuki is not strictly based on a hereditary system. In fact, the case of the Ichikawa Danjūrō family, which continued to the ninth generation mostly through its blood line, is an exception. During the Edo period, it was more common for an actor to adopt a promising student and have him

相続が増えたのは明治以降で、歌舞伎俳優の世間的地位が江戸時代より向上したことの現れと言えるでしょう。

歌舞伎俳優の家に生まれた子供は、ほとんどが6歳ごろには日本舞踊、長唄、三味線などの稽古を始めます。ここに歌舞伎俳優の家に生まれた子供の利点があるといえます。日本舞踊は特に重要視されています。

かといって外部の世界から歌舞伎俳優になる道が閉ざされているわけではありません。現在では、個人的に俳優に弟子入りする方法と国立劇場の歌舞伎俳優養成研修を受ける方法の2通りがあります。国立劇場では、中学校卒業以上の男性を対象に2年間の研修が行われます。歌舞伎俳優や舞踊家などが指導に当たり、卒業後は歌舞伎俳優の元に弟子入りし、プロとして活動します。同劇場では、鳴物、長唄などの音楽演奏者の研修も行っています。

歌舞伎の上演劇場

 歌舞伎はどこで見られますか。

A 東京の歌舞伎専門劇場には、歌舞伎座と国立劇場があります。歌舞伎座では通年、国立劇場では年間7ヵ月の歌舞伎公演が行われています。この他に三越劇場や浅草公会堂、

succeed the line. Transmission via one's blood relatives became more common only after the Meiji period. This may be due to the fact that the social status of kabuki actors, which had been very low, became somewhat higher during the Edo period.

Most children born into kabuki families start their training in *nihon buyō*, or Japanese classical dance, *nagauta*, shamisen, and other arts, when they are six. Special emphasis is placed on the art of classical dance. This is one of the advantages of being born into a kabuki family.

On the other hand, this does not mean that the door is shut to aspiring actors not born into a kabuki family. At present, there are two paths to becoming a professional kabuki actor. The first is to apprentice oneself to an established actor, and the other is to enroll in a kabuki actors' training program given by the National Theater, which offers a two-year training for boys who have finished middle school. There, the students are given guidance by kabuki actors and *buyō* dancers. After graduation, they will apprentice themselves to established actors and begin working professionally. The same theater also offers training for would-be musicians in playing the *narimono* and the *nagauta*.

KABUKI THEATER

Q Where can one see kabuki?

In Tōkyō, playhouses built specially for kabuki are Kabuki-za and the National Theater. Performances are held in Kabuki-za throughout the year, and seven months of the year at the National Theater. In addition, shows may be held at the

新橋演舞場などで公演が行われることもあり
ます。大阪では松竹座、京都では南座、名古
屋では御園座で年間数公演があります。1999
年6月には福岡に博多座が開場し、ここでも
年に数回の歌舞伎公演が行われることになる
ようです。このほかに文化庁主催の巡業公演
などがあります。

郵 便 は が き

112-8790

料金受取人払

小石川局承認

3565

差出有効期間
平成14年3月
31日まで

東京都文京区音羽一丁目
十七番十四号

講談社
インターナショナル　行
愛読者カード係

|||ı|l·||·ıı|ıı|ı·||·ı||ı·ıı···ı·|ı|·ı·|ı|·ı·|ı|·ı·|ı|ı·ıı|ıı|||||

★この本についてお気づきの点、ご感想などをお教えください。

本のタイトルを
お書きください

愛読者カード

ご愛読ありがとうございました。下の項目についてご意見をお聞かせ
頂きたく、ご記入のうえご投函くださいますようお願いいたします。

a　ご住所　　　　　　　　　　　　〒□□□-□□□□

b　お名前　　　　　　　　　　　　年齢 （　　　）歳

　　　　　　　　　　　　　　　　性別　1 男性　2 女性

c　ご職業　1 生徒・学生 （小、中、高、大、その他）　2 会社員
　　　　　3 自営(商工、農林漁、サービス、その他)　4 公務員　5 教職員
　　　　　6 自由業(　　　　　　　　　)　7 無職(主婦、家事手伝い、その他)
　　　　　8 その他(　　　　　　　　　)

d　本書をどこでお知りになりましたか。
　　　1 新聞広告（新聞名　　　　　　）　2 雑誌広告(雑誌名　　　　　　)
　　　3 書評(書名　　　　　　)　4 実物を見て　5 人にすすめられて
　　　6 その他(　　　　　　　　　)

e　どんな本を対訳で読みたいか、お教えください。

f　どんな分野の英語学習書を読みたいか、お教えください。

御協力ありがとうございました。

Mitsukoshi theater, Asakusa Kōkaidō, Shinbashi Enbujō and other places. Ōsaka has Shōchiku-za, Kyōto has Minami-za, and there are several performances a year held at Misono-za, in Nagoya. In June 1999, Hakata-za opened in Fukuoka, and it plans to hold kabuki shows several times a year. Apart from this, there are provincial tour performances sponsored by the Ministry of Culture.

能・狂言
Nō and Kyōgen

能の始まりと発展

 一口に言って、能・狂言とはどんなものですか。

能(井筒)

A 能・狂言は、歌舞伎などにも大きな影響を与えた日本の伝統芸能の源流です。能は室町時代に完成し、戦乱や時代の変化を乗り越えて現在にまで至っています。

「謡」と呼ばれる語り、「仕舞」と呼ばれる舞い、そして囃子(演奏)が一体となって1つの世界を作り出します。省略を重ねた舞台、無駄を殺ぎ落とした象徴的な演技、幻想性が強いストーリーなど、芸術的に高い完成度を持っており、また、能面や能装束の美しさも見る人を惹き付けます。

狂言(附子)

狂言は能の間に上演されることが多く、能と共に発展してきました。能舞台で演じますが、能のように仮面を用いることは少なく、セリフを主体にした喜劇です。現実的なストーリーが多く、動きも写実的でわかりやすいものです。

歌舞伎が時の政府からしばしば弾圧されて来たのに対して、能は、将軍家や大名など権力者に愛され、保護を受けてきました。謡は武士の教養の1つとしてたしなまれ、誕生してから600年が経過した現在でも、愛好する

ORIGINS AND DEVELOPMENT OF NŌ

Q Defined simply, what are nō and kyōgen?

Nō and kyōgen represent a wellspring for traditional Japanese performing arts and, as such, they have had tremendous influence on kabuki and other arts that developed later. Perfected in Japan's Muromachi period (1333–1568), nō has survived intact the subsequent years of war and social upheaval and is still performed today.

Nō created a new theatrical world by fusing three genres: narrative songs called *utai*, a form of dance called *shimai*, and musical accompaniment called *hayashi*. With a story containing strong elements of the fantastic, a richly symbolic performance pared to the barest essentials, a stage stripped to the most basic elements, nō attains the highest levels of artistic perfection. Added to this, the beauty of the nō masks and costumes transfixes the eye.

Kyōgen, which developed together with nō, is often performed in the intervals between nō plays. Though kyōgen is performed on the nō stage, unlike nō, masks are seldom used and dialogue is the central part of the comical performances. Both the kyōgen stories and performances tend to be realistic and easy to understand.

While kabuki was often suppressed by the government, nō was both prized and protected by the shōgun and other military leaders. The performance of nō *utai* was long considered to be an important part of the cultural accomplishments of the samurai and, even today, more than 600 years after the birth

人がたくさんいます。

Q 能は、いつ、どこで誕生したのでしょうか。

A 能の源となるものは、平安時代から鎌倉時代にかけて栄えた「猿楽」という芸能です。

猿楽

猿楽

猿楽は鎌倉時代になると、ほかの芸能の影響を受けて発達し、鎌倉中期には「座」という猿楽を演じる劇団が誕生しました。中でも有力だったのが大和国(奈良県)の大和猿楽で、ここには現在のシテ方4流儀の祖となる結崎、外山、円満井、坂戸の4座がありました。能を今日の形に大成させたのも、結崎座に所属した観阿弥と世阿弥の親子です。

Q 観阿弥とはどんな人だったのでしょうか。

A 観阿弥は南北朝時代の元弘3(1333)年に生まれました。芸名が観世、法名が観阿弥陀仏で、観阿弥はその略称です。観阿弥は作者と能役者を兼ね、後の観世派となった結崎座の初代座長(大夫)として京都に進出し、室町幕府の三代将軍・足利義満の後援を受け、他の座を圧倒する力を持つようになります。

当時、盛んな芸能に、田植えの祭礼から発

of nō, there are many people who perform *utai* for their own personal enjoyment.

Q When and where was nō born?

The origins of nō can be found in the *sarugaku* performances that developed in the Heian period (794–1185) and Kamakura periods (1185–1333).

In the Kamakura period, *sarugaku* developed under the influence of other performing arts, and by the middle of the period, *sarugaku* theatrical troupes, known as *za*, had been formed. Among the most important of these were the Yuzaki, Tobi, Enman'i, and Sakado troupes which performed Yamato-style *sarugaku* in the Yamato region (Nara Prefecture). These four troupes are the ancestors of four of the *shite kata* (principal player) schools of nō actors that exist today. Kan'ami and his son Zeami, the two people who brought nō to the form that is still performed today, were members of the Yuzaki troupe.

Q What kind of person was Kan'ami?

Born in Genko 3 (1333), Kan'ami's stage name was Kanze. The name Kan'ami itself is an abbreviation of his Buddhist name Kan'amidabutsu. Both a playwright and an actor, Kan'ami moved to Kyōto as the first leader of the Yūzaki troupe, which later became the Kanze school. After obtaining the patronage of Ashikaga Yoshimitsu, third shōgun of the Muromachi shogunate, Kan'ami came to have power far exceeding that of the other nō troupes.

One performing art already in existence in Kan'ami's time

田楽

自然居士

したと見られる「田楽」がありました。音楽に合わせて楽しげに歌い、踊る芸能で、猿楽がメロディーに優れていたのに対し、田楽はリズムに長所がありました。観阿弥は物まね主体だった猿楽に、この田楽などから歌や踊りの要素を取り込み、優美さを加味し、芸術性を高めました。亡くなったのは至徳元(1384)年。代表作に「自然居士」、「卒都婆小町」などがあります。

Q 世阿弥は能にどんな功績があったのでしょうか。

A 世阿弥は観阿弥の子の二代目観世大夫で、貞治2(1363)年ごろに生まれたと言われます。法名は世阿弥陀仏です。幼いころの名を藤若と言います。

世阿弥は、父の死を受けて観世座を相続し、技芸を磨きました。彼は際立った美貌を持ち、足利義満の寵愛を受けました。四代将軍の義持にも高い評価を受けましたが、五代将軍の義教は、世阿弥の甥の音阿弥をひいきして、世阿弥を迫害し、彼を佐渡島へ流罪としました。世阿弥は流罪が許された後の嘉吉3(1443)年に没したと言われますが、正確な没年は不明です。

そういう不幸な生涯でしたが、世阿弥は観阿弥の能をさらに洗練させました。謡曲の作者として卓越した才能を持ち、傑作を次々と

was *dengaku*, which is thought to have developed from performances at festivals associated with rice planting. Of the arts that involved merrily dancing and singing to music, *sarugaku* was considered superior from the standpoint of melody, while the strong point of *dengaku* was thought to be its rhythm. Kan'ami incorporated elements of the songs and dances of *dengaku* and other arts into *sarugaku*, which had previously been focused on the portrayal of characters. At the same time, he added elegance and artistry to the performances. Kan'ami's best known plays include *Jinen Koji* and *Sotoba Komachi*. He died in Shitoku 1 (1384).

Q What were Zeami's achievements in nō?

Born around Jōji 2 (1363), Zeami was the son of Kan'ami and became the second head of the Kanze school. His Buddhist name was Zeamidabutsu, and as a child he was called Fujiwaka.

After his father's death, Zeami took over the direction of the Kanze school and refined its techniques. Strikingly handsome, Zeami was favored by shōgun Ashikaga Yoshimitsu. He was also judged highly by Yoshimochi, the fourth Ashikaga shōgun, but the fifth shōgun, Ashikaga Yoshinori, was partial to Zeami's nephew On'ami and persecuted Zeami, exiling him to the island of Sado. Zeami was later allowed to return from exile, and he is said to have died in Kakitsu 3 (1443), but the exact year is not known.

Despite the ill fortune he experienced, Zeami was able to further refine the nō he inherited from Kan'ami. Zeami was a preeminent nō playwright, producing masterpiece after master-

高砂

書きました。代表作は「高砂」、「敦盛」、「班女」、「桜川」、「砧」、「井筒」などなど多数です。作品の多くの題材は「平家物語」や「伊勢物語」などの古典文学からとられています。

　世阿弥は「夢幻能」を完成させたことでも有名です。夢幻能とは、主人公を実在する人物ではなく、霊として登場させる手法で、「高砂」がその1つです。

　彼はまた理論家でもあり、能楽の理論書を執筆しました。「風姿花伝」や「申楽談儀」などは、能の教科書としてだけではなく、すぐれた演劇書として、今も読み継がれています。

　中でも「風姿花伝」は世阿弥が書いた最初の能楽の理論書で、「花伝書」とも言います。能役者の年齢に応じた修業の仕方や、演技の方法などを解説しています。

　彼は、舞台の上の役者の美しさなどを「花」に例えました。若くて美貌の役者が輝くような魅力を発揮することを「時分の花」と名付けました。また、「秘すれば花」という言葉も有名です。芸の秘密は隠しているからこそ価値があるという意味です。

 　観阿弥、世阿弥の後、能はどのように発展したのですか。

　A 大和猿楽の4座は「結崎」が「観世」、「外山」が「宝生」、「坂戸」が「金剛」、「円満井」が「金春」にとそれぞれ、能の4つの

piece. Among his many famous plays are *Takasago*, *Atsumori*, *Hanjo*, *Sakuragawa*, *Kinuta*, and *Izutsu*. A large number of his plays are based on works of classical literature, such as *Heike Monogatari* (*The Tale of the Heike*) and *Ise Monogatari* (*Tales of Ise*).

Zeami is also famous for perfecting *mugen* nō (dream nō), in which the main character appears as a spirit rather than as a living person. The play *Takasago* is one example.

Zeami excelled as a theorist, penning a number of theoretical treatises on nō. *Fūshi Kaden* (Transmission of the Flower of Acting Style) and *Sarugaku Dangi* (Conversations on *Sarugaku*), are two such treatises studied even today, not only as textbooks of nō but also as brilliant essays on drama.

Fūshi Kaden was the first theoretical treatise on nō that Zeami wrote; it is also known as *Kadensho*. In this work, he comments on acting techniques and considers the ways in which an actor's training should be geared to his age.

Zeami likened the beauty created by the actor on the stage to a flower. Zeami called the young and beautiful actor giving full play to his shining appeal on stage *jibun no hana* (flower of the season). Another famous term of Zeami's is *hisureba hana* (flower of mystery), meaning that the secret of an art becomes all the more valuable for its being hidden.

 How did nō develop after Kan'ami and Zeami?

The four Yamato *sarugaku* troupes evolved into four schools of nō. The Yūzaki troupe became the Kanze school; the Tobi troupe, the Hōshō school; the Sakado troupe, the

流派へと発展しました。当初、4座の中で一番勢力を持ったのが、将軍家に愛された観世座でした。

世阿弥の子で達人と言われた観世元雅は、「隅田川」や「弱法師」などの傑作を残しましたが、早死にし、音阿弥が観世座を継ぐことになりました。六代将軍義教にもうとんじられていた世阿弥は、その後、島流しになりました。その音阿弥と共に当時の猿楽の能の発展に寄与したのが、世阿弥の娘婿で金春座を率いた金春禅竹です。禅竹は世阿弥の教えを引き継ぎ、金春座を観世座に対抗するような大勢力としました。

弱法師

やがて、1467年に、11年にも及ぶ応仁の乱が勃発し、室町時代は戦国の乱世となって行きます。戦国大名の多くは、それぞれに能役者を抱えました。1590年に天下統一を果たした豊臣秀吉も能を愛し、自分でも舞を楽しんだほどで、4座を保護しました。将軍となった徳川家康も能を好み、能は江戸幕府の式典の際の芸能として保護されました。二代将軍秀忠の時には、4座に加えて、「喜多流」が幕府から許されて創設され、以来、現在まで、そのすべてが存在しています。

しかし、江戸時代の能は、大名などの武家や富裕な町人などの限られた層に愛好され、

Kongō school; and the Enman'i troupe, the Komparu school. Initially, the most powerful of the four schools was the Kanze school because it was favored by the Muromachi shōguns.

Zeami's talented son Kanze Motomasa wrote masterpieces such as *Sumidagawa* and *Yoroboshi*. When he died in his mid thirties, On'ami became head of the Kanze school. Zeami, out of favor with the sixth shōgun, Yoshinori, was subsequently exiled to Sado. Another person who, along with On'ami, contributed to the development of *sarugaku* nō at this time was Komparu Zenchiku, leader of the Komparu school and son-in-law of Zeami. Zenchiku followed the teachings of Zeami and developed the Komparu school into a strong rival of the Kanze school.

In 1467, the eleven years of conflict known as the Ōnin Wars began, initiating a period of civil strife that lasted for the final century of the Muromachi period. This century is also known as the *Sengoku*, or Warring States, period (1467–1568). Many of the *sengoku daimyo* (feudal lords) supported nō actors in their own domains. Toyotomi Hideyoshi, the warlord who reunified the country in 1590, was a great aficionado of nō. He supported the four nō schools, and he delighted in performing in nō plays himself. The first Tokugawa shōgun, Ieyasu, also enjoyed nō, which was subsequently protected as an official ceremonial art of the Tokugawa shogunate. During the time of the second Tokugawa shōgun, Hidetada, the shogunate permitted the establishment of the Kita school, bringing the total number of major schools of professional nō actors to five, all of which are still in existence today.

Although nō was supported by the shogunate, during the Edo period (1600–1868) the common people for the most part

庶民とは離れたところにある芸能でした。町
人は本格的な能ではなく、「謡」の一節を流行
歌のように口ずさんで楽しむのが一般でした。

やがて明治維新となり、江戸幕府が崩壊し、
能も幕府や大名の保護を受けることができな
くなり、廃業した役者も多く出ます。しかし、
維新の混乱がおさまったころ、政府の高官が
海外を視察し、オペラや演劇が手厚く処遇さ
れている文化状況を目の当たりにして帰国
し、日本でも古典芸能を保護することにしま
した。能もこうした動きから息を吹き返し、
各流派が舞台を独自に作り、能の会などを催
すようになりました。一般の人が謡や舞を習
う機会も増え、能も広く普及しました。

能の演目

 能の作品はどんな題材で作られているのですか。

A 「平家物語」などの源平合戦の戦記、
「伊勢物語」「大和物語」などの古典文学、そ
れに「古今和歌集」などの歌集から題材を取
った作品がほとんどです。

lost interest in it, and its popularity was limited to certain groups, such as samurai clans, including the *daimyo*, and wealthy merchants. Townspeople may have enjoyed singing refrains from *utai* (nō songs) as they would a popular tune, but in general they showed little interest in nō as a full-fledged theater art.

With the Meiji Restoration in 1868, the Tokugawa shogunate crumbled, and nō lost the support of both the feudal government and the *daimyo*. This led many nō actors to quit the profession. Once the confusion of the Restoration began to settle, however, government officials went on fact-finding tours abroad and saw for themselves the cultural environment and the warm reception given to opera and drama performances. When these officials returned home, they decided to protect Japan's own classical performing arts. This helped breathe life back into nō, and the various nō schools built their own nō theaters and established groups to promote nō. Opportunities increased for the average citizen to study nō songs and dances, and nō became widely known in society.

THE NŌ PERFORMANCE PROGRAM

 What kind of subject matter is used as the basis for nō plays?

The subject matter of almost all nō plays is taken from *Heike Monogatari* (*The Tale of the Heike*) and other military tales of the war between the Genji and Heike clans, as well as from works of classical literature such as *Ise Monogatari* (*Tales of Ise*) and *Yamato Monogatari* (*Tales of Yamato*), and

　その内容は「脇能物(初番目物)」、「修羅物」、「鬘物」、「雑物」、「切能物」の5種類に分類できます。

　能のプログラムを「番組」と言いますが、江戸時代の能は、上の5種類の順番で、5つの作品が上演されるのが基本でした。現在では5つの上演はまれで、能を二、三番に、狂言を一番という番組が一般的です。

　「脇能物」は神や、神に近い人物が主題で、「神能物」とも呼ばれます。ある神社が出来た由来などを、主人公である神の化身が説き明かすといった内容が多く見られます。代表的な作品に「高砂」「養老」などがあります。

清経

　「修羅物」は脇能物に続いて上演されることが多かったので「二番目物」とも言われます。修羅物では主人公はおおむね男性の武将で、生前に戦に参加した罪によって死後は、苦しみを味わっています。「田村」以外はすべて源平合戦で活躍した武将で、経てきた戦の苦難について物語ります。「敦盛」「清経」「朝長」などが有名です。

　「鬘物」は3番目に上演されたので「三番目物」とも言われます。ほとんどの場合、女性が主人公で頭に鬘をつけるためにこの名がつ

from poetry anthologies such as the *Kokin Wakashū* (A Collection of Japanese Poems from Ancient and Modern Times).

The content of nō plays can be broken down into the following five categories: *waki nō mono* (plays emphasizing *waki*), also called *shobamme-mono* (part-one plays); *shura-mono* (warrior plays); *kazura-mono* (wig plays); *zatsu-mono* (miscellaneous plays); and *kiri nō mono* (final nō plays).

In the nō program (called the *bangumi*) of the Edo period, it was standard to present a play in each of the above five categories in the order given. It is now rare for five plays to be presented. A program today generally consists of two or three nō plays along with one kyōgen piece.

Because *waki nō mono* have a god or godlike person as their subject, they are sometimes referred to as *kami nō mono* (god plays). In many of these plays the main character, who is the personification of a god, explains the origins of a shrine. Representative works in this category include *Takasago* and *Yōrō*.

Shura-mono are also called *nibamme-mono* (part-two plays) since they traditionally appeared second in the program, following the *waki nō mono*. The main character in *shura-mono* is almost always a military officer who, after dying, is tormented by the sins he committed during battle. All the plays in this category except *Tamura* are tales of the bitter war experiences of generals involved in the war between the Genji and Heike clans. Famous plays here include *Atsumori*, *Kiyotsune*, and *Tomonaga*.

Kazura-mono traditionally appeared third in the program, giving rise to the name *sambamme-mono* (part-three plays). The reason this category is labeled *kazura-mono* (wig plays) is

きました。しばしば美女の霊が登場し、昔を
しのんで優雅な舞を舞います。能が追い求め
た「幽玄」と言われる優雅さが最もよく表現
されるのが鬘物です。鬘物には人気作品が多
く「井筒」「熊野」「大原御幸」「吉野天人」
「夕顔」「羽衣」などが有名です。

「雑物」は4番目に上演されることが多いの
で「四番目物」とも言われます。ほかの4つ
に分類されないものがここに入ります。その
中でいちばん多いのが「狂女物」、あるいは
「狂乱物」です。子や夫を失った女性が狂乱
の様子を見せるものです。「班女」「雲雀山」
「蝉丸」「隅田川」「卒都婆小町」などがそう
です。男の狂乱物の「高野物狂」や、「現在
物」と言われる、面をつけないで素顔のまま
で演ずるものもここに分類されます。

「切能物」は5番立てでは最後に上演される
ため、「五番目物」とも呼ばれます。多くは
鬼や亡霊など人間にとって恐ろしいものを主
人公にしている作品です。「土蜘蛛」「紅葉狩」
「殺生石」「春日竜神」などがそうです。
　この5番を順に「神」「男」「女」「狂」「鬼」
と言いますが、唯一どこにも分類されない作
品が「翁」です。

that the main character is almost always a woman, so the actor must wear a wig. Often the spirit of a beautiful woman appears. As she recalls the past, she performs an elegant dance. The quality of *yūgen* (elegance) that nō seeks to engender is expressed most clearly in plays in this category. Many popular plays can be found here, including *Izutsu*, *Yuya*, *Ohara Gokō*, *Yoshino Tennin*, *Yūgao*, and *Hagoromo*.

Zatsu-mono are also called *yobamme-mono* (part-four plays) since they were traditionally performed fourth in the program. Plays that do not fall under any of the other four categories are included here. The most common of this type of play is the *kyōjo-mono* (mad woman play), also called the *kyōran-mono* (madness play). In these plays a woman who has lost her husband or child takes on the appearance of madness. Examples include *Hanjo*, *Hibariyama*, *Semimaru*, *Sumidagawa*, and *Sotoba Komachi*. *Kōya Monogurui*, a madness play with a male lead character, is also a *zatsu-mono* as are a number of *genzai-mono* (present-day or realistic plays) in which the actors do not wear masks.

The plays appearing last in the traditional program, *kiri nō mono*, are also called *gobamme-mono* (part-five plays). The main characters in many of these plays are frightening demons and spirits. Such plays include *Tsuchigumo*, *Momijigari*, *Sesshōseki*, and *Kasuga Ryūjin*.

This five-category sequence is referred to overall as *shin-nan-jo-kyō-ki* (god-man-woman-lunatic-demon), although there is one play, *Okina*, which does not fall into any of the five categories.

Q 「翁」という作品は「能にして能にあらず」と
言われるそうですが、一体どんな作品なのでしょうか。

翁

A 正式名称は「式三番」です。「能にして能
にあらず」と言われる通り、他の能とは異な
り筋らしい筋はありません。祝言に演じる儀
式的な3つの曲を言います。古くからあった芸能
が猿楽と結び付いたものと考えられます。

「式三番」への出演者は、食事の煮炊きの火
を家族と別にするなど、身を清めるのがしき
たりでした。それほど神聖視されていた演目
だったわけです。

Q 世阿弥の完成した「夢幻能」とは
どんな内容なのでしょうか。

A 能は、霊など、実在しないものが主人公
で過去を回想するものと、主人公を霊ではな
く実在する人物として登場させるものの2つ
に大きく分けられます。前者を「夢幻能」と
言い、後者を「現在能」と言います。

「夢幻能」では、神や霊である主人公が、旅
人などに昔のことを話します。最初はありふ
れた人間の姿を借りて現れ、次には、昔の姿
や本当の姿になって登場します。「シテ」と
呼ばれる主役の演技が中心に置かれ、「ワキ」
と呼ばれる脇役はシテの話を引き出すための
演技をします。

ワキの見た夢や幻であるという設定で、作
品が成立しているために「夢幻能」と名付け

Q The play *Okina* is known as being "nō and yet not nō." What kind of work is it?

The official name of this play is *Shikisanba*. As is implied by its "nō and yet not nō" reputation, *Okina* is different from other nō plays, the difference being that it does not have a plot. Its three ceremonial songs are like celebratory prayers. This ancient entertainment is thought to be related to *sarugaku*.

The performers appearing in *Shikisanba* traditionally purified themselves through rituals such as cooking their food separate from other family members. This shows the strong sacred aspect of *Okina*.

Q What kind of plays are found in *mugen* nō (dream nō), perfected by Zeami?

Nō can be divided overall into those plays in which the main character is a spirit, or other supernatural entity who reflects on past events, and those plays in which the main character appears as a real person rather than a spirit. The former of these two types is referred to as *mugen* nō, while the latter is called *genzai* nō (present-day or realistic nō).

In *mugen* nō, the god or spirit who is the main character speaks to another character, often a traveler, of the events of the past. Initially, this god or spirit appears in ordinary human form, after which the character appears in his or her old form or true form. The central focus of these plays is the performance of this main character, who is called the *shite*. The supporting character, called the *waki*, is there to draw out the speech of the *shite*.

The label *mugen* nō (dream nō) was given because the premise on which these plays operate is that the *shite* is a

られています。前の質問で分類した「脇能物」「修羅物」「鬘物」の多くがこの夢幻能です。世阿弥は夢幻能の傑作をたくさん世に送り出したのです。

　一方、「現在能」に登場する人物のほとんどは生きている人間で、夢幻能と異なり、シテだけではなく、脇役も活躍します。親子や男女の情愛とそれに伴う苦悩が綴られている作品や武士の勇気などを描いた作品が多くみられます。曾我兄弟の仇討ちを描いた「夜討曾我」や源義経の若き日である牛若丸の活躍を描いた「烏帽子折」などが代表的です。

演者の役割と能の構成

Q シテとかワキとか、いろいろな役者が登場しますが、舞台の上で、それぞれどんな役割をしているのでしょうか。

シテ

A 簡単に言えば、能の主役がシテ、脇役がワキです。シテで作品の前半に出てくるのを前ジテ、後半に出てくるのを後ジテと言います。前ジテと後ジテは同一人物が引っ込んで再登場する場合もあれば、「船弁慶」のように前が源義経の恋人の静御前、後が平知盛の霊であるというぐあいに、まったく異なる人物である場合もあります。シテは、他に「ツレ」と呼ばれる、シテに伴ってその演技を助

dream or apparition seen by the *waki*. Many of the plays in the aforementioned *waki nō mono*, *shura-mono*, and *kazura-mono* categories are considered to be *mugen* nō. Zeami himself created many masterpieces of *mugen* nō.

In *genzai* nō, on the other hand, almost all the characters are living human beings. In addition, unlike *mugen* nō, not only the *shite* but also the supporting *waki* character generally plays a significant role. Many of these plays tell of the love and accompanying hardships in relationships between men and women or between parents and children, and many are tales of warrior courage. Representative examples include *Youchi Soga*, which tells of the vengeance of the Soga brothers, and *Eboshiori*, which portrays the exploits of warrior Minamoto no Yoshitsune when he was a child and known as Ushiwakamaru.

THE STRUCTURE OF NŌ AND THE ACTORS' ROLES

Q There are various types of actors, such as the *shite* and *waki*, in nō plays. How does each role on the stage?

Put simply, the main character in nō is called the *shite* and the supporting character is called the *waki*. The main character as he/she appears in the first half of the play is called the *maejite* (before *shite*), and the main character as he/she appears in the second half is called the *nochijite* (after *shite*). In some plays the *maejite* and *nochijite* are the same character, and in others they are totally different characters. An example of the latter type is the play *Funa Benkei*, which has Minamoto no Yoshitsune's lover Shizuka Gozen as the *maejite* and the spirit

ける役と共に登場する場合もあります。

　ワキはシテと異なり、ほとんどが生身の人間として舞台に登場し、必ず男性です。夢幻能ではワキが最初に登場して、状況の説明を行い、シテが出てきてからは、その演技を助けます。ワキは能面を付けることはありません。ワキがツレを連れてくる場合もあり、それは「ワキヅレ」といいます。

シテ（中央）

　能の演者はシテ方、ワキ方、囃子方、狂言方に分かれ、シテはシテ方、ワキはワキ方から出るのが決まりです。シテ方が観世、宝生、金春、金剛、喜多の5流です。ワキ方には宝生（脇宝生
と呼びます）、福王、高安の3流があります。
　ほかに「子方」と言って少年の演じる役があります。これはシテ方の子供が出る決まりで、その登場の仕方には2種類あります。1つが、芝居の子役と同じように少年の役を演じる場合。そしてもう1つが、大人の役を子供が演じる場合です。「安宅」や「船弁慶」の義経、「大仏供養」の頼朝などがそうです。子供が演じることにより、役柄の象徴性を高める効果があると言われています。子方も能面はつけません。
　能でコーラスのように数人で舞台に並び、謡曲を語る人々を「地謡」といいますが、こちらもシテ方から出ます。

地謡

of Heike warrior Taira no Tomomori as the *nochijite*. The *shite* sometimes appears together with a character called the *tsure*. The role of the *tsure* is to assist the *shite*.

Unlike the *shite*, almost all *waki* appear on stage as living human characters, and they are always men. In *mugen* nō, the *waki* appears first to explain the circumstances and then supports the *shite* role after the *shite* appears. *Waki* do not wear masks. In some plays the *waki* brings in a *tsure* character known as the *wakizure*.

Nō performers are classified as *shite kata* (principal players), *waki kata* (supporting players), *hayashikata* (musicians), and kyōgen *kata* (kyōgen players). Actors for *shite* roles are chosen from among the *shite kata*, while actors for the *waki* roles, from among the *waki kata*. The five *shite kata* schools are Kanze, Hōshō, Komparu, Kongō, and Kita. The three *waki kata* schools are Hōshō (called Waki Hōshō), Fukuō, and Takayasu.

There are also *kokata* (child roles) played by child actors. The children of the *shite kata* are chosen for these parts. There are two ways in which child actors appear in nō plays. They may play child characters or adult characters. Examples of the latter include the Yoshitsune roles in *Ataka* and *Funa Benkei* and the Yoritomo role in *Daibutsu Kuyō*. The use of a child actor is said to have the effect of increasing the symbolic aspect of the role. Child actors do not wear masks.

The nō chorus, called the *jiutai*, is lined up at the side of the stage, from where it sings the nō songs. Chorus members come from the *shite kata* schools.

後見

　舞台に作り物を運び込んだり、シテの装束を整えたりする「後見」も重要です。後見は通常2人で、舞台の後座の左の隅に座り、演者に目を光らせています。演者が言葉に詰まったときは後ろでセリフを教えたり、演能中に急病になったりした場合には、後見が即座に変わります。それだけの高い技量を求められるわけです。「道成寺」のような大曲の場合には、シテ方のほか狂言方、囃子方にも後見が多くつきます。

 能はどのような構成で作られているのでしょうか。

　A 能のテキストを謡曲と言います。役者と地謡の歌う歌詞を書いたものです。
　謡曲は「序・破・急」で構成されます。始めはゆったりと重々しく、次第にテンポを上げ、最後は急速に終えます。この「序破急」は能のすべてを統御する原理です。1つの作品はもとより、5番立ての構成自体が、脇能物が序、修羅物と鬘物と雑物が破、切能物が急と、「序破急」にあてはめることができます。

　1つの作品では、ワキが登場して場所に付くまでが序、シテ(主人公)が現れるのが破の一段、ワキとシテのやりとりが破の二段、シテの物語から中入りを破の三段、後ジテの場面を急とします。

The *kōken* (stage assistants), who carry the set pieces on stage and adjust the costume of the *shite*, have a number of important functions. There are usually two *kōken*; they sit at the back left corner of the stage and closely watch the actors. If an actor forgets his lines, the kōken prompts him, and if an actor suddenly becomes ill, the *kōken* will immediately take his place. This shows the high level of skill required of the *kōken*. In a large-scale play such as *Dōjōji*, there are *kōken* for the musicians and kyōgen actors as well as for the *shite*.

 How are nō plays structured?

The nō text is called the *yōkyoku*. In it are written the lyrics sung by the actors and chorus.

The *yōkyoku* has a three-part structure: *jo* (introduction), *ha* (exposition), and *kyū* (rapid finale). The beginning is composed and solemn; in the middle the tempo increases gradually, and the ending moves quickly. This *jo-ha-kyū* pattern is a basic principle controlling all of nō. Single plays follow the pattern as does the traditional five-play program. In the nō *jo-ha-kyū* program, the *waki nō mono* is the *jo*; the *shura-mono*, *kazura-mono*, and *zatsu-mono* are the three parts of the *ha*; and the *kiri nō mono* is the *kyū*.

In a single play, *jo* covers the period up until the *waki* appears and reaches the appointed location. The appearance of the *shite* marks the first part of the *ha*, the exchange between the *waki* and *shite* constitutes the second part of *ha*, and the period that begins with the telling of the *shite*'s story and ends with his temporary exit is the third part of the *ha*. The *kyū* is

能の舞台

 能舞台はいつごろ出来たのでしょうか。

能楽堂

 能を演じる劇場を「能楽堂（のうがくどう）」と言います。能楽堂は能舞台と客席（「見所（けんしょ）」と呼ばれます）から構成されています。現在のような舞台の形式が完成したのが、室町時代の末と言われています。しかし、江戸時代の末までは、能舞台は屋外に作られるものでした。中でも、江戸城の本丸に作られた舞台が最高の格式を持ち、五代将軍綱吉の時代には、城内に7つもの能舞台があったそうです。

 能舞台はどんな構造になっているのですか。

 能舞台は6メートル四方の大きさで四隅には柱が立ててあり、その上に屋根がついています。外にあった名残で、屋内にもかかわらず、屋根があるわけです。後方には、「後座（あとざ）」と呼ばれる囃子方や後見が座る場所が、右手には地謡座が付き、後座の左側から斜めに「橋掛り（はしがかり）」という、手摺のついた廊下が延びています。

　4本の柱の内、手前左を目付柱（めつけばしら）、手前右を

when the *nochijite* (after *shite*) performs.

THE NŌ STAGE

 Around when was the nō stage created?

The stage on which nō performances take place is called the *nōgakudo*. The *nōgakudo* comprises the nō stage and the audience seating area, called the *kensho*. It is said that the nō stage, in a form similar to that which exists today, was perfected at the end of the Muromachi period (1333–1568). Until the end of the Edo period (1600–1868), however, the nō stage was constructed outdoors. The stage with the highest status during this period was the one built in the main enclosure (*hommaru*) of Edo castle. During the time of the fifth Tokugawa shōgun, Tsunayoshi, there were purportedly seven nō stages in the Edo castle grounds.

 What is the structure of the nō stage?

The nō stage is six by six meters, with a pillar in each corner and a roof above. Even if a nō stage is indoors, it still has the roof as a vestige of the time when all stages were outdoors. To the back of the stage is the *atoza* (rear stage) area, where the musicians and stage assistants sit. To the right, facing the stage, is the *jiutaiza*, the area where the chorus sits. Extending on a diagonal from the back left corner is the *hashigakari* (bridge), a corridor with hand rails.

The four pillars all have names: at left front is the *metsuke-*

ワキ柱、奥の右側を笛柱、奥の左側をシテ柱といいます。目付柱は演者が、この柱を目安にして位置を確かめて舞うことから名が付いた重要度の高いものです。ワキ柱とシテ柱は、ワキ方、シテ方が近くに座るために名が付き、笛柱は囃子方のうちで、笛方が近くに座るために名が付きました。笛柱にだけ、金環がありますが、これは「道成寺」で鐘を天井に吊るすためにのみ使われます。

橋掛り

能舞台平面図

後座

舞台

後座の後ろの壁は「鏡板」と呼ばれ、大きな松が描かれています。右奥には、切戸口という小さな出入り口があり、後見や地謡は切戸口から出入りします。舞台正面には小さな梯子があり「キザハシ」と呼びますが、現在では使用しません。

橋掛りは手摺のついた廊下で、突き当たりに演者の出入り口の揚幕があります。演者は揚幕から橋掛りを通って舞台に登場します。橋掛りは通路であると同時に舞台の一部でもあります。

揚幕の奥は、「鏡の間」という大きな鏡が置かれた場所で、楽屋で衣装などを付けた演者はここで床几（いす）に腰掛け、鏡に向かい能面を付け、精神を統一します。舞台の裏側には楽屋があり、シテ方、ワキ方、狂言方、囃子方に分かれています。

舞台の前方が正面、目付柱から左側を中正

bashira (eye-fixing pillar), at right front is the *waki-bashira* (subordinate actor's pillar), at left rear is the *shite-bashira* (principal actor's pillar), and at right rear is the *fue-bashira* (flute pillar). The eye-fixing pillar is an important part of the physical stage; it received this name because the actors use it as a landmark for checking their position on stage. The *shite* and *waki* pillars received their names because the respective characters sit near them. The flute pillar got its name because the flute player, who is one of the *hayashikata* (musicians), sits nearby. On the flute pillar is a gold ring not found on the other pillars. The ring is only used for suspending a bell from the ceiling in the play *Dōjōji*.

The wall at the rear of the stage is called the *kagamiita* (mirror board); it has a large pine tree painted on it. At the right rear is a small door called the *kiridoguchi* (sliding door), which is used by the stage assistants and chorus. At the front of the stage are small steps, called the *kizahashi*, no longer used in performances today.

At the far end of the *hashigakari* is the *agemaku* (curtain), through which the performers enter and exit. Actors go through the curtain and cross the *hashigakari* to get to the main stage. The *hashigakari* itself is both a passageway to the stage and a part of the stage.

Beyond the curtain is the *kagami no ma* (mirror room), which has large mirrors installed. Here the actor, who has already dressed in the *gakuya* (dressing rooms), sits on a small folding stool in front of the mirror and puts on his mask and composes his spirit. Behind the stage are separate dressing rooms for the *shite*, *waki*, kyōgen, and child performers.

The area in front of the stage is called the *shōmen*, the area

面、橋掛りの前を脇正面といいます。舞台と見所の間には白い小石を敷きつめた庭のようなスペースがあり、ここを「白洲」といいます。橋掛りの横にも白洲があり、ここには3本の松の木が植わっています。舞台に近い方から一ノ松、二ノ松、三ノ松と名が付いています。

能舞台

能の音楽

Q 囃子方はどんな楽器を演奏するのでしょうか。

A 大鼓、小鼓、笛、太鼓の4種類があり、「四拍子」と呼ばれます。笛と太鼓は座って、大鼓と小鼓は床几にかけて演奏します。後座の前に、右から笛、小鼓、大鼓、太鼓の順に並びます。

囃子方

大鼓

小鼓

大鼓は桜で出来た胴に馬革を張って、調緒という麻の紐で締めてあります。小鼓も桜材に馬革製です。この大小の鼓は謡の中のリズムをリードします。大鼓は強く激しい音色、また小鼓は優しく柔らかい音色です。

笛は竹製の横笛で、能管といいます。能で

to the left of the *metsuke-bashira* is called the *nakajōmen*, and the area in front of the *hashigakari* is called the *waki-shōmen*. The space between the stage and the audience is a garden-like area covered by small white stones, called the *shirasu* (strip of pebbles). There are three pine trees planted in the part of the *shirasu* that runs in front of the *hashigakari*. Beginning from the one closest to the stage, they are called the *ichi no matsu* (first pine), *ni no matsu* (second pine), and *san no matsu* (third pine).

NŌ MUSIC

 What instruments do the *hayashikata* (musicians) play?

There are four types of instruments: *ōtsuzumi* (large hand drum), *kotsuzumi* (small hand drum), *fue* (flute), and *taiko* (large drum). Collectively, the instruments are known as the *shibyōshi*. The *fue* and *taiko* players perform sitting on the floor; the *ōtsuzumi* and *kotsuzumi* players perform sitting on small folding stools. The instruments are lined up from right to left (facing the stage) across the front part of the *atoza* (rear stage) area in the following order: *fue*, *kotsuzumi*, *ōtsuzumi*, and *taiko*.

The *ōtsuzumi* is made of a cherry wood shell and horsehide heads. The latter are tightened with a hemp cord called the *shirabeo*. The *kotsuzumi* is also made with cherry wood and horsehide heads. These two drums maintain the rhythm of the songs. The *ōtsuzumi* produces a sharp, resonant crack, and the *kotsuzumi*, a softer, gentler thump.

The nō flute is made of bamboo and is called the *nōkan*. It

笛

は旋律を奏でる唯一の楽器です。演奏者の技術のうまい、へたによって音色は異なります。

太鼓

太鼓は、神や人間以外の霊、鬼などをシテとする能に用いることが多く、こうした能を特に「太鼓物」といいます。牛革製で、台に載せて打ちます。能のクライマックスで打つ場合が多いようです。

能ではこうした楽器のことを「道具」といいます。

Q 謡とはどんなものなのでしょうか。

A 謡はコトバとフシ、つまり、セリフとメロディーに分かれます。

フシの発声は、強く息を扱う「強吟」と、弱く息を扱う「弱吟」に分けられます。勇壮な場面では強吟、哀愁を帯びた場面では弱吟を使います。

能のリズムを「乗」といいます。乗には「平ノリ」「中ノリ」「大ノリ」の3種類があります。平ノリは謡では最も一般的なノリです。七五調の12字を8拍に当てはめてあります。大ノリは1字1拍、中ノリは2字1拍です。大ノリは、霊が登場した後など、中ノリは霊が恨みを言う時などに多く使います。それ以外のほとんどは平ノリです。

シテ、ワキ、ツレが登場して最初に謡うのが、その役の意向や感慨などを述べる「次第」です。「七五」「七五」「七四」の3句(2句目は1

is the only instrument in nō that can play a melody. The timbre of the sound produced varies depending on the skill of the performer.

Because the *taiko* is in many cases used for nō plays in which the *shite* appears as a god, a non-human spirit, or demon, these plays are sometimes referred to as *taiko-mono* (*taiko* plays). This drum is made with cowhide and sits on a low stand. It is frequently played at the climax of a nō play.

The ensemble of instruments used in nō are called *dōgu* (tools).

 ## What are the *utai* (songs) like?

A song can be divided into the words and the melody. The vocalization of the melody can be done in two ways: a strong style, called *tsuyogin*, and a weaker style, called *yowagin*. *Tsuyogin* is used in heroic scenes and *yowagin* in sorrowful scenes.

Rhythm in nō is referred to as *nori*. There are three types of *nori*: *hira-nori*, *chū-nori*, and *ō-nori*. Of these, *hira-nori* is the most frequently used; it distributes the twelve syllables of a seven-plus-five syllable line over eight beats. *Ō-nori* has one syllable per beat, and *chū-nori* has two syllables per beat. *Ō-nori* is often used after a spirit has appeared, and *chū-nori* is often used when a spirit is speaking of its bitterness or anger. At other times, *hira-nori* is almost always used.

In the *shidai* (entrance song), performed by the *shite*, *waki*, and *tsure* when they first appear on stage, the character speaks of his intentions or emotions. The verse consists of three lines

句の繰り返し)からなる韻文です。地謡はこの次第を繰り返します。「安宅」の「旅の衣は篠懸の、旅の衣は篠懸の、露けき袖やしおるらん」などがこれに当たります。

曲の中心になる謡が「クセ(曲)」です。室町時代に流行した鼓に合わせて歌う叙事的な歌謡「曲舞」の略で、その技法を取り入れたものです。シテが戦いの物語をする場面などで、クセとなります。大半は地謡が語り、シテは「居グセ」といって、座っている場合と、「舞グセ」といって、立って舞う場合とがあります。

クライマックスで謡うのが「狂イ」です。「狂い地」ともいい、狂女などが、心を乱して舞う際に謡います。平ノリ、弱吟で緩急を付けて切迫した様を表現します。

of seven-plus-five, seven-plus-five, and seven-plus-four syllables, with the second line being a repeat of the first. The chorus repeats the *shidai*. An example of a *shidai* from the play *Ataka* is:

> *Tabi no koromo wa suzukake no.*
> (Traveling in ascetic's robes.)
> *Tabi no koromo wa suzukake no.*
> (Traveling in ascetic's robes.)
> *Tsuyukeki sode ya shioruran.*
> (Sleeves wet with dew and tears.)

The principal song of the nō play is called the *kuse*. This is a shortened form of the term *kusemai*, which was the name of a genre of narrative songs sung with drum accompaniment, popular in the Muromachi period (1333–1568). The techniques of *kusemai* were adopted in the nō *kuse*. An example of a *kuse* would be a song in which the *shite* tells the tale of a battle. The majority of *kuse* are sung by the chorus. A *kuse* where the *shite* is sitting is called an *iguse* (sitting *kuse*), and one where the *shite* is dancing is called a *maiguse* (dancing *kuse*).

The song performed at the climax of a nō play is called the *kurui* or *kuruichi*, words that can mean "derangement" or "madness." This song is sung, for example, when a mad woman dances in a disturbed mental state. The strain and tension of the character is expressed by changes in pace achieved using a *hira-nori* rhythm and *yowagin* style.

能面、装束と小道具

Q 能面にはどんな種類があるのでしょうか。

小面

A 能は仮面劇だと言われます。しかし、舞台に出る全員がつけるわけではなく、能面はシテとツレが使います。

能面の特徴は、喜怒哀楽の表現が曖昧に作られていることです。ところが、顔につけて、うつむいたり、あお向いたり、様々な動きをすることによって、変化のないはずの能面に、あらゆる感情が生まれてくるのです。

能面は基本的には60種類ぐらいに分けられます。

増女

女面は能面の中でも人気の高い物です。最も若い女性の面が「小面」で、ほかに若い女性には「孫次郎」「増女」「若女」などがあります。

老女

中年の女性には「深井」など、高齢の女性には「姥」「老女」を用います。どの作品にどの面を使うかは演者や流儀によって変わってきます。

中将

男面には、中年の武将の「平太」、貴公子の「中将」「今若」、半僧半俗の少年の面の「喝食」などがあります。「敦盛」「景清」「弱法師」にはその作品専用の面がありますが、ほとんどは使い回しです。

翁

「翁」は穏和な笑顔の老人の面です。祝福を

NŌ MASKS, COSTUMES, AND STAGE PROPERTIES

 Q What types of nō masks are there?

Nō is considered a form of mask drama, even though all the players on stage do not wear masks. Nō masks are worn by the *shite* and *tsure*.

A defining characteristic of the nō mask is the way in which the emotion it expresses is made to be ambiguous. When it is put on, however, the theoretically static mask is able to express a wide range of feelings through various movements and the way its gaze is angled slightly down or up.

Fundamentally, nō masks can be categorized into about sixty types.

Masks depicting young women represent some very popular types. The "youngest" female mask is the *ko-omote*; other young-woman masks include the *magojirō*, *zō-onna*, and *waka-onna*.

The *fukai* is one of the masks used for middle-aged women. Those used for old women include the *uba* and *rōjo*. The mask used in a given play varies depending on the actor and the school.

Male-character masks include the *heita* (middle-aged warrior mask), the *chūjo* and *imawaka* (young-nobleman masks), and the *kasshiki* mask for a young male role that has both secular and religious aspects. Most masks are used in multiple plays, although some, such as the *atsumori*, *kagekiyo*, and *yoroboshi* masks, are used only in the plays bearing these same names.

The *okina* mask portrays the placid smiling face of an old

表す面、神の面とされています。

痩男

　怨霊の面に使うのが、男性の場合は、地獄に落ちて苦しみのためにやせ衰えた霊を表す「痩男(やせおとこ)」、「蛙(かわず)」など。女性の場合は、同じく「痩女(やせおんな)」、「霊女(りょうのおんな)」、嫉妬に狂った美女の生き霊を表す面「泥眼(でいがん)」、そして「般若(はんにゃ)」などがあります。般若の面は、女の恨みと悲しみをこめたものとして、特に有名です。

般若

　このほかにお酒の好きな妖精の「猩々(しょうじょう)」、山に住む鬼女の「山姥(やまうば)」などもあります。

Q 能の衣装は随分豪華に見えますが、どんな種類がありますか。

　A 能や狂言では衣装のことを「装束(しょうぞく)」といいます。能装束は室町時代の日常の服装から発展し、舞台衣装として完成して行きました。最初は材質なども質素だったのが、次第に豪華な物になっていったようです。特に江戸時代には、大名たちは自分たちが後援する能役者に、競って豪華な装束を与えました。

唐織

　装束としては、頭につける「仮髪(かはつ)」という鬘、烏帽子(えぼし)などの冠(かずら)り物、上衣(うわぎ)、着付(きつけ)と言われる上衣の下に着る小袖、袴(はかま)などがあります。

　豪華な装束には、絹の色糸を使った「唐織(からおり)」

man. It is considered to be the mask of a god and to express divine blessings.

There are a number of masks for vengeful spirits. For men, these include the *yase-otoko* and *kawazu* masks depicting spirits starved and weakened by the torments of hell. For women there are the *yase-onna* and *ryō no onna* masks, with gaunt features similar to the aforementioned male masks, and the *deigan* mask, which depicts the living spirit of a woman driven mad by jealousy. The *hannya* mask is particularly famous as a mask embodying a woman's hatred and sorrow.

Other masks include the *shōjō* mask depicting a fabulous creature who loves saké, and the *yamamba* mask depicting a mountain witch.

 Nō costumes look truly magnificent.
What kinds of costumes are there?

Costumes for nō and kyōgen are referred to as *shōzoku*, which means "costume" or "attire." Nō stage costumes developed out of the everyday clothing worn in the Muromachi period (1333–1568). Initially, the materials used were quite plain, but they gradually became more and more extravagant. During the Edo period (1600–1868) especially, the feudal lords competed with each other in giving splendid costumes to the nō actors whom they supported.

Among the costumes used in nō are wigs, called *kahatsu*; headgear, such as the *eboshi* hats worn by court nobles; and *uwagi* (jackets). *Kitsuke* (nō clothing) includes *kosode* (a type of small-sleeved kimono) and *hakama* (loose-fitting trousers), both worn under the *uwagi*.

Among the more luxurious costumes are those of *karaori*

などがあります。

　装束では色も重要な意味を持ちます。特に「紅色（赤色）」がポイントで、「紅色」のある衣装が「色入り」、無いものが「色無し」と称されています。「色入り」は、「熊野」や「松風」のシテなど若い女性に用い、「色無し」は「隅田川」「三井寺」などの中年の女性に用います。

　襟の色もまた重要な意味を持っています。白が最も高貴で、赤は白より位が下です。身分の低い役柄には萌葱を用います。

鬘帯

　女性の役は必ず鬘をつけます。黒髪を真ん中から分けて後ろで結んだものが一般的で、上に鬘帯という鉢巻をしめます。長い鬘を「長鬘」と言って、狂った女性などの役に使います。鬘の毛を前へ垂らしたのを「付髪」といいます。

　なお、能役者はすべて、白足袋を履くのが決まりです。

Q 舞台装置や小道具にはどんなものがありますか。

　A 能では歌舞伎のような写実的な装置を使うことはしません。演技と同様に装置も極めて簡略化され、象徴的なものになっています。ほとんどは骨格を竹で作って、白い布で巻いてあるだけです。「船弁慶」の船、「熊野」の車、「紅葉狩」の山、「三井寺」の鐘楼などすべてこの形式です。たいていの場合は、後見

brocade, made with colored silk thread.

The color used in a costume has an important meaning, with the use of red being particularly significant. Costumes with red are said to be *iro-iri* (with color), while those without red are said to be *iro-nashi* (without color). *Iro-iri* examples include young-woman characters such as the *shite* in *Yuya* and *Matsukaze*. *Iro-nashi* examples include the middle-aged-woman characters in *Sumidagawa* and *Miidera*.

The color of the under-kimono *eri* (neckband) also carries important meaning. White indicates the highest dignity, red indicates somewhat less dignity than white, and yellowish green is used for people of low status.

A wig is always worn for female roles. The general practice is for black hair to be parted in the center and tied in back, with a headband called a *katsura obi* (wig band) tied on top. Long-haired wigs, called *nagakazura* are used for mad woman roles. A wig with hair hanging in front is called a *tsukegami*.

All nō actors wear white *tabi* (Japanese socks).

Q What kinds of stage sets and properties are there?

Nō does not use realistic stage sets such as those found in kabuki. Similar to the acting style, the stage set is distilled down to a sparse and symbolic minimum. In most cases there is only a bamboo framework wrapped with white cloth. The boat in *Funa Benkei*, the carriage in *Yuya*, the mountain in *Momijigari*, and the bell tower in *Miidera* are all made in this way. Usually the stage assistants carry the construction in and

中啓

が、能の開始時に、舞台に運んで据え置きます。

演者に限らず、囃子方、地謡、後見なども含めた全員が持っているのが扇です。扇には閉じた時にも先が開いた形になる「中啓」、全体が閉じる「鎮扇」の2種類があります。演じる役柄や流儀によって、使う扇の種類も異なります。

能の演技の基本

Q 舞などの動きにはどんな種類がありますか。

カマエ

A 姿勢の基本となるのが、立ち姿の「カマエ(構エ)」です。やや前傾した姿勢で、背筋を延ばしたまま、重心を低くします。男女や役柄に応じて、カマエは少しずつ異なります。

歩く動作を「ハコビ(運ビ)」といいます。能では体が上下に動くことを嫌い、どんなに急いでいる時でも、かかとを上げず、床に足の裏を付けて摺り足で進みます。役者は足袋しか履きません。

サシコミ

足で舞台の床を踏んで拍子を取るのが「足拍子」です。音を立てる場合と立てない場合があります。7回以上踏むのを「数拍子」といいます。

扇を持った右手を下から体の前に出しなが

place it on the stage at the beginning of the play.

Everyone onstage, including not only the actors but also the musicians, chorus members, and stage assistants, carry a folding fan. There are two categories of folding fans used: the *chūkei*, which is slightly open at the end, even when closed; and the *shizumeōgi*, which can be fully closed. The type of fan used also varies depending on the nō school and the role.

THE BASICS OF NŌ PERFORMANCE

 Q **What types of movements are there in nō dancing and other elements of the performance?**

The basic nō posture is an upright posture called the *kamae*. The upper body is tilted slightly forward with the back straight; the body's center of gravity is kept low. The *kamae* varies somewhat between male and female characters and between roles.

The walking movement is called the *hakobi*. In nō, vertical up-and-down movement of the body while walking is rigorously avoided. Even when a character is supposed to be hurrying, the foot glides with the sole in contact with the floor and without raising the heel. The actors wear only *tabi* (Japanese socks) on their feet.

Beating time on the stage floor with an actor's footfalls is called *ashibyōshi* (foot rhythm). In some cases sound is deliberately made, and in others it is deliberately avoided. To step seven times or more is referred to as *kazubyōshi* (number rhythm).

Movement forward as the right hand carrying the folding

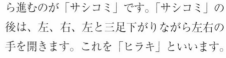

ヒラキ

ら進むのが「サシコミ」です。「サシコミ」の後は、左、右、左と三足下がりながら左右の手を開きます。これを「ヒラキ」といいます。

片手を目にあてて涙を押さえる型を「シオリ」といいます。もっと激しく泣く時は両手で目を押さえます。これを「モロジオリ」といいます。

シオリ

驚きの表現で、両腕を広げ、そして両手を胸の前で合わせるのが「ウチ合ワセ」。扇を広げて胸の前で上下させるのを「ユウケン」といい、喜びの表現などに使います。

扇を使う表現はほかにもたくさんあります。扇で顔の左側を隠すと、恥ずかしさを表現します。広げた扇を額の左側にあててうつむくと、眠っていることを表します。横に広げた扇を上下させれば、人を招き寄せる動作です。

モロジオリ

舞は、「二人静」や「小袖曾我」のように二人一緒に舞うこともあり、これを「相舞（あいまい）」と呼びます。武士がさっそうと速い動きで舞うことを「男舞（おとこまい）」といい、笛、小鼓、大鼓で伴奏をします。「安宅」の弁慶の「延年（えんねん）の舞」が特に有名です。

ウチ合ワセ

舞に似ているけれど、舞のような抽象的、様式的な動きではなく、特定の意味のある動作をすることを「働（はたらき）」と言っています。例えば、笛、小鼓、大鼓の演奏のもとで、戦闘の

fan is lifted and thrust in front of the body is called *sashikomi*. After *sashikomi*, moving three steps back (left, right, left) while opening both arms is called *hiraki*.

The placing of one hand over the eyes as if to hold back tears is called *shiori*. More intense tears are signified by placing both hands over the eyes; this is called *morojiori*.

Expressing surprise by holding out both arms and bringing both hands together in front of the chest is called *uchiawase*. Opening the fan and moving it up and down in front of the chest is called *yūken*; this is an expression of joy.

There are many other things expressed using the folding fan. Holding the fan over the left side of the face shows embarrassment. Holding an open fan against the left forehead and looking downward indicates the character is sleeping. The up and down movement of an open fan held to the side is done to beckon someone.

The main type of dance in nō is called *mai*. *Mai* in which two characters dance together, as in the plays *Futari Shizuka* and *Kosode Soga*, are referred to as *aimai* (together dances). *Mai* in which a warrior dances gallantly with fast movements are called *otokomai* (men's dances). These have *fue* (flute), *kotsuzumi* (small hand drum), and *ōtsuzumi* (large hand drum) accompaniment. A famous example of an *otokomai* is the *ennen* (longevity) dance of the Benkei character in the play *Ataka*.

Another category of movement, called *hataraki*, is similar to *mai*. The movements of *hataraki* have a specific meaning and are not as abstract and stylized as those of *mai*. One example of *hataraki* is the *kakeri* type, in which a dance expressing

ユウケン

有り様や苦しみ、狂乱の興奮状態などを表現するのが「カケリ」、放心とか、人を尋ね求める雰囲気を表すために、舞台を一回りするのが「イロエ」です。僧などが霊や鬼女などを祈り伏せる姿を表す「イノリ」もあります。「葵上（あおいのうえ）」などにもこれを用います。

能役者たちの世界

 能役者や囃子方は世襲ですか。

A 5流派や観世流の梅若家（うめわか）や観世流の分家の鉄之丞家（てつのじょう）のように室町、江戸の時代から代々続く家柄もありますが、各流派に弟子入りして能役者になっている人も、ことにシテ方には多くいます。

シテ方に比べてワキ方、囃子方、狂言方に進む人は少ないため、国立能楽堂では昭和59 (1984)年から、ワキ方、囃子方、狂言方の後継者を育成するための研修制度を始めました。研修期間は6年間で、3年ごとに募集しています。

the conditions, hardship, and mad excitement of battle is done to *fue*, *kotsuzumi*, and *ōtsuzumi* accompaniment. Other examples include the *iroe* type, in which the dancer circles the stage to show an abstracted state of mind or to express the desire that someone visit, and the *inori* (prayer) type, in which a monk tries to subdue a spirit or female demon. There is an *inori* dance in the play *Aoi No Ue*.

THE WORLD OF THE NŌ ACTOR

 Are the positions of the actors and musicians in nō hereditary?

There are nō family lines, such as those in the five nō schools. The Umewaka family and Tetsunojō family branch of the Kanze school have lineages extending across many generations, from the Muromachi period (1333–1568) through the Edo period (1600–1868) until today. Each nō school, however, also accepts new pupils from outside for training as nō actors, particularly for *shite* roles.

Compared to the number of people training to be *shite* actors, there are few training as *hayashikata* (musicians) or as *waki* or kyōgen actors. For this reason, in 1984, the National Nō Theater began a program for training a new generation of *hayashikata* as well as *waki* and kyōgen actors. The training period is six years. New students are accepted every three years.

Q **能・狂言はどこへ行けば見られるのでしょうか。**

> **A** 能舞台は全国各地にあり、その数は50を
> 超します。特に東京には、観世、宝生などの
> 各流派が能楽堂を構えていますし、昭和58
> (1983)年には国立能楽堂も完成して、毎月多
> くの公演が行われています。
>
> このほかに屋外での火を焚いての「薪能」
> や、ホールでの狂言会なども開かれています。

狂言

 Q **狂言はいつごろ、どうやって成立したのでしょうか。**

狂言

> **A** 狂言も能と同様に「猿楽」の中に含まれ、
> 明治になるまでは、「猿楽の狂言」と呼ばれ
> ていました。明治に入り、「猿楽」は「能」
> と呼ばれるようになります。一方の狂言は、
> 歌舞伎の作品のことも「狂言」といったので、
> 区別をつけるために「能狂言」と称されまし
> た。現在は「狂言」といえば、歌舞伎ではな
> く、この「能狂言」を指すのが一般的です。
>
> 能の項でも書きましたが、能も元は滑稽な
> 演技から出発したものでした。狂言も同じ
> 「猿楽」から発生し、室町時代に能と共に発
> 展していったようです。織田信長、豊臣秀吉
> は能同様に狂言も保護しました。
>
> 江戸時代になると狂言方はワキ方、囃子方

Q What is the outlook for nō and kyōgen in the future?

There are over fifty nō stages located throughout the country. In Tōkyō, in particular, there are many nō performances every month since nō schools such as Kanze and Hosho have theaters there. Added to this, the National Nō Theater was built in Tōkyō in 1983.

There are also torchlight performances of nō, called *takigi* (firewood) nō, which are held outdoors in the evening. Kyōgen associations sometimes hold performances in public halls.

KYŌGEN

Q When and how did kyōgen develop?

As was the case with nō, kyōgen was originally considered part of *sarugaku*. In fact, until the Meiji period (1868–1912), it was known as *sarugaku no kyōgen*. In the Meiji period, *sarugaku* came to be called nō. Kyōgen, on the other hand, came to be called nō kyōgen because the word kyōgen was also used to refer to kabuki plays at that time. Today, however, the term kyōgen used by itself generally refers to nō kyōgen rather than to kabuki.

As was mentioned earlier in the section on nō, nō has its origins in comical *sarugaku* performances. Kyōgen, with the same origins, developed along with nō in the Muromachi period (1333–1568). Both were supported by the warlords Oda Nobunaga and Toyotomi Hideyoshi.

In the Edo period (1600–1868), kyōgen *kata* (kyōgen play-

と共に能のシテ方の支配下に組み込まれます。大蔵流、鷺流の2流派が幕府のお抱え狂言師として江戸で活躍し、和泉流は朝廷や尾張藩、紀州藩のお抱え狂言師として、勢力を延ばしました。

明治維新で、能・狂言は突然、権力者の保護から離れることとなります。鷺流が衰え、大正時代に滅んでしまったのもそうした状況の1つの現れです。能は国を代表する演劇として早くに評価されるようになりましたが、「喜劇」である狂言は軍事国家にあっては一段低くみられました。そんな中で狂言師は地道な活動を続け、普及につとめました。

 狂言方にはどんな流派があるのでしょうか。

A 鷺流が滅び、現在あるのは大蔵流と和泉流の2流です。大蔵流は宗家が明治時代に絶え、現在は東京の山本家と関西の茂山家の2派が力を持っています。和泉流も大正時代に宗家が絶えましたが、弟子筋の三宅藤九郎家の流れを汲む野村万蔵家から三宅家に養子が入り、さらにそこから和泉家を継承しています。

ers) as well as *waki kata* (supporting players) and *hayashikata* (musicians) came to be subordinate to the nō *shite kata* (principal players). During this period, the Okura and Sagi schools of kyōgen prospered under the direct patronage of the Tokugawa shogunate, while the Izumi school flourished with the support of the imperial court and the Owari and Kishu domains.

With the Meiji Restoration in 1868, both nō and kyōgen suddenly lost the protection of the powers that be. One result of this state of affairs was the decline of the Sagi school and, in the Taisho period (1912–1926), its disappearance. Nō was quickly recognized and esteemed as a representative theater art of Japan. The "comic theater" kyōgen, however, was somewhat looked down upon under the military government. In this atmosphere, kyōgen actors continued to work steadily to increase the popularity of their art.

 What schools of kyōgen are in existence today?

The end of the Sagi school left two schools remaining: Ōkura and Izumi. In the Ōkura school, the principal family lines died out in the Meiji period. The main groups today are the Yamamoto family in Tōkyō and the Shigeyama family in the Kansai region. Similarly, the Izumi school's principal family lines died out in the Taishō period (1912–1926). When a member of the Nomura Manzō family, a branch of the Miyake Tokurō family, was adopted into the Miyake family, the Izumi family got a new start.

狂言師は能の中ではどんな役割をするのでしょうか。

A 「間狂言」に出演することで、「アイ（間）」と表記します。間狂言は「語り間」と「アシライ間」に分けられます。「語り間」は夢幻能、「アシライ間」は現在能に多くみられます。

語り間の中で座って語る形式のものを「居語り」といいます。シテが中入りで退場した後に、土地の住人などに扮したアイが、ワキの質問に答えて、その土地にまつわる物語を語り聞かせます。夢幻能は2場からなり、前ジテと後ジテは多くの場合に同じ演者がつとめます。それには装束を変える時間が必要で、その間をつなぐために、狂言方が登場するようになったわけです。

最初は立ったままワキと話す形式だったのが、次第に「語り」の部分が増え、座った状態の居語りに発展したようです。「高砂」「井筒」などで居語りが見られます。

アシライ間は能の中の主要な役をアイがすることです。「道成寺」の寺男、「安宅」の富樫の従者など、シテやワキの従者などを演じる場合が多く、しっかりしたシテやワキにはない人間味あふれる失敗をして物語の進行に一役買います。

例えば、「道成寺」の寺男は女性が入ることを禁じられている寺に、実は魔物である

Q **What kind of roles do kyōgen actors have in nō plays?**

When the kyōgen actor performs a narrative or skit within a nō play, it is called *aikyōgen* (intermission kyōgen) or just *ai*.

Aikyōgen is classified into two types: *katariai* and *ashiraiai*. *Katariai* are frequently found in *mugen* nō, and *ashiraiai* are frequently found in *genzai* nō.

Instances of *katariai* in which the actor sits and recites his speech are called *igatari*. After the *shite* leaves the stage there is an interval between acts. During this interval the *aikyōgen* actor, often portraying a local villager, replies to a question of the *waki* by telling the story of what happened there. In *mugen* nō there are two acts, and the same actor usually plays both the *maejite* (before *shite*) and *nochijite* (after *shite*). This actor, of course, needs time to change costume. The kyōgen actor thus came to be used in this interval to link the two acts.

Initially, the kyōgen actor would stand and speak to the *waki* in a form called *tachi-shaberi* (standing chat). Subsequently and gradually the narrative portion increased, developing into the *igatari* type of sitting narrative. These *igatari* can be seen in the plays *Takasago* and *Izutsu*.

With *ashiraiai*, the *aikyōgen* actor appears in an important role within the nō play itself. In many cases, the role is that of an attendant to the *shite* or *waki* character, examples being the temple servants in *Dōjōji* and the attendant of the barrier-station guard Togashi in *Ataka*. These characters help advance the plot, and the blunders they sometimes make can give them a humanity not found in the *shite* and *waki*.

In Dōjōji, for example, the temple servants set in motion the play's plot by allowing a female dancer, who turns out to

白拍子を入れてしまい、大騒動のきっかけを
作ります。能の最初に登場し、事情を説明す
る場合もあり「口開け間」といいます。

Q 狂言独自の作品にはどんな種類があるのでしょうか。

A 狂言には260種類ぐらいの曲数があると
いわれ、そのほとんどが「喜劇」です。人気
のある作品を、ジャンル別に書き出してみま
しょう。

神様の出るのが脇狂言で「福の神」「大黒
連歌」などがあります。

人のいい大名を主人公とするのが大名物で
代表作は「鬼瓦」「蚊相撲」など。

太郎冠者などの召使いを主人公とするの
が小名物で代表作は「素袍落」「棒縛」「附子」
など。

聟を主人公にしたのが聟物で代表作は「二
人袴」「船渡聟」など。

恐妻家の夫や妻を欲しがっている男を主人
公にしたのが女物で、代表作は「釣針」「鎌
腹」など。

鎌腹

山伏が活躍するのが山伏物で代表作は「柿
山伏」「菌」など。

鬼や閻魔大王などが登場するのが鬼物で代
表作は「節分」「朝比奈」など。

僧侶が主役なのが出家物で代表作は「宗論」
「無布施経」など。

be a demon, into a temple where women are prohibited from entering. In some nō plays, a kyōgen actor will appear at the beginning of the play to explain the background of the story; this is called *kuchiake ai* (opening *ai*).

 ## What types of independent kyōgen plays are there?

There are said to be about two hundred and sixty kyōgen plays, and almost all of them are comedies. Play categories and one or two popular examples of each are listed below.

Plays in which a god appears. This category is called *waki* kyōgen. Popular examples include *Fuku No Kami* and *Daikoku Renga*.

Plays in which the main character is a gullible *daimyō* (feudal lord). Examples: *Onigawara* and *Kazumō*.

Plays in which the main character is a servant named Tarō Kaja. Examples: *Suō-otoshi*, *Bōshibari*, and *Busu*.

Plays in which the main character is a son-in-law or *muko* (bridegroom). Examples: *Nininbakama* and *Funawatashi Muko*.

Plays in which the main character is a henpecked husband or a man looking for a wife. Examples: *Tsuribari* and *Kamabara*.

Plays in which a *yamabushi* (mountain ascetic) appears. Examples: *Kaki Yamabushi* and *Kusabira*.

Plays in which an *oni* (demon) or Emma, the lord of hell, appear. Examples: *Setsubun* and *Asahina*.

Plays in which the main character is a Buddhist priest. Examples: *Shūron* and *Fuse Nai Kyō*.

目の不自由な人が主人公になるのが座頭物で代表作は「月見座頭」など。

農民が主役なのが百姓物で代表作は「佐渡狐」など。

以上に属さない集狂言には「瓜盗人」「茶壺」などがあります。

同じ題材でも、狂言は流派によって演じ方や筋が異なります。観阿弥や世阿弥のような大作者の名前も残ってはいません。代々の狂言役者が書き、演じ方を工夫してきたものと考えられ、能以上に流派による相違は大きいのです。能と違い大曲は少なく、上演時間も40分以内の曲がほとんどです。

 太郎冠者という人物がよく出てきますが、どんな人物ですか。

A 種類からも分かるように狂言の主役となるのは、能と異なり、たいていが庶民階級です。大名であっても、一国一城の主というよりは、地主程度に考えた方がいいような親しみの持てる人物がほとんどです。

よく登場するのが太郎冠者です。太郎冠者は主人に使える家来です。大名からある命令を下された太郎冠者が、失敗したり、怠けたりすることによって生じる滑稽な騒動が主題となる狂言はたくさんあります。例えば「附子」。出演するのは太郎冠者、次郎冠者と主

Plays in which the main character is a blind person. Example: *Tsukimi Zatō*.

Plays in which the main character is a farmer. Example: *Sadogitsune*.

Plays that do not fit into the above categories are included in a miscellaneous category called *atsume* kyōgen. Examples include *Uri Nusubito* and *Chatsubo*.

Although it has the same subject matter, a given play performed by different schools will show variations both in the plot and the performance style. There are no major kyōgen playwrights, such as Kan'ami and Zeami in nō, whose names are still known today. Kyōgen plays are thought to have been written by generations of kyōgen actors, who also developed a performance style. Variations between schools in kyōgen are greater than in nō. Unlike nō, there are few long plays in kyōgen, with most being performed in under forty minutes.

 The character Tarō Kaja appears often. What kind of person is he?

Unlike in nō, in many cases the main character in a kyōgen play is an ordinary person. Even when the main character is a *daimyō*, rather than being the remote, powerful head of a major domain, he almost always is a more approachable character, on the order of a local landowner.

One frequently appearing ordinary person is Tarō Kaja, who is a servant working for his master. There are many plays in which the principal subject is the comical disturbance created as a result of the mistakes and laziness of Tarō Kaja when he tries to carry out an order from his master. One example is the play *Busu*, which has three characters: Tarō Kaja, Jirō Kaja

人。小名物に当たります。

太郎冠者と次郎冠者は外出する主人から、附子の入った瓶を預けられます。附子は猛毒だから、気をつけるようにと主人から言い残され、怯えていた2人ですが、好奇心から瓶に近寄り、食べてみて実は砂糖と知り、たいらげてしまいます。2人は主人の掛け軸を破り、茶碗を割ります。帰宅して驚く主人に、2人は誤って掛け軸と茶碗を損なったので、お詫びに死のうと附子を食べたが死ねなかったと言い訳し、怒った主人に追いかけられます。

「附子」の
太郎冠者と次郎冠者

Q 狂言の主役もシテ、脇役をワキと言うのですか。

A 狂言の主役のことは能と同様にシテといいますが、脇役のことはワキではなく、アドと呼びます。アドが2人以上登場する時は、主アド、次アド、三のアドと順位をつけた言い方をします。アドがたくさん出る時は、全員を「立衆」と総称します。

狂言はたいていの場合に最初の登場人物が、自己紹介する「名ノリ」から始まります。そこへ他の人物が登場して物語が展開し、最後はアドがシテを「やるまいぞ、やるまいぞ」と追いかけて入る形式が一般的です。

(another servant), and their master.

Tarō Kaja and Jirō Kaja are given a jar of *busu*, a kind of poison, to take care of by their master, who must go out for a while. He reminds them to be careful since *busu* is a deadly poison. This frightens the two servants, but, overcome with curiosity, they approach the jar and have a taste. It turns out to be sugar, and they end up eating it all. Then they tear their master's hanging scroll and break his bowl. Their master is shocked when he returns home, but the servants explain that to atone for having damaged the scroll and bowl by mistake, they tried to kill themselves by eating the *busu*, yet they didn't die. The two are then chased around the stage by their angry master.

 Q **Is the main character in kyōgen called the *shite* and the supporting character the *waki*?**

The main character in kyōgen is called the *shite*, the same as in nō, but the supporting character is called the *ado* rather than the *waki*. When more than one *ado* appear in the same play, they are named in sequence of appearance: first *ado*, second *ado*, and third *ado*. When many *ado* appear in a play, they are collectively called the *tachishū*.

Generally in kyōgen, the first character that appears on stage begins with a *nanori* (self-introduction). The other characters then come on stage and the story proceeds. A common ending is for the *ado* to chase the *shite* off the stage shouting "I won't let you get away! I won't let you get away!"

Q 狂言のセリフや謡は能に比べて
随分と分かりやすいような気がします。
どんな特徴があるのでしょうか。

「ドブ、ドブ」

「ズカ、ズカ」

A 狂言のセリフは、能と違って口語体がほとんどです。発生当時の室町時代末から江戸時代前期までの日常語が基礎になっているといわれています。ですから、現代人が聞いても、そのほとんどの意味を理解することができます。

狂言独特の言語表現としては演者が口でいう擬音があります。酒を杯につぐ動作の時には「ドブ、ドブ」と声を出し、空になった表現では「ピショ、ピショ」と声を出します。鋸で木を引く時には「ズカ、ズカ」といいます。物を破る時には「メリメリメリ」と表現します。

Q 狂言の演出にはどんな特徴がありますか。

A 「カマエ」「ハコビ」などは能と共通です。流派によって歩き方なども微妙に違いますが一般に強い役柄ほど、歩幅を大きくします。「釣狐」のシテは狐で、人間に化けて登場します。この場合は爪先を床から離さないで歩くのが特徴です。笑う場合でも太郎冠者などよりは大名の方が大げさに笑います。

先程の擬音語でも分かるように狂言には写実と様式が共存しています。泣く場面では能では「シオリ」といって片手を目にあてて涙

The dialogue in kyōgen seems a lot easier to understand than in nō. Does the kyōgen dialogue represent the colloquial speech of that period?

Unlike nō, kyōgen dialogue is almost all in colloquial language. It is said to be based on the everyday speech of an era running from the late Muromachi period (1333–1568) to the early Edo period (1600–1868). For this reason, contemporary Japanese can understand the meaning of most of what is said.

Kyōgen actors produce onomatopoeic sound effects that are unique to kyōgen. When an actor is mimicking pouring saké into a saké cup he says, *dobu, dobu*. To show the container is empty, he says *pisho, pisho*. The expression when cutting wood with a saw is *zuka, zuka*, and when tearing something, *meri meri meri*.

 What are the characteristics of the kyōgen actor's performance?

Techniques such as the *kamae* posture and the *hakobi* walking method are the same as in nō. Walking methods and other techniques vary subtly between kyōgen schools but, in general, the stronger the role, the longer the stride. The *shite* in *Tsurigitsune* is a fox who appears as a human. This role has a characteristic walk in which the tips of the toes are not raised off the floor. Laughing methods also vary, with the *daimyō* having a more exaggerated laugh than commoners such as Tarō Kaja.

Kyōgen's use of onomatopoeic effects, as discussed in the answer to a previous question, shows that realistic and stylistic elements coexist in kyōgen. In nō, crying is expressed through

を押さえる素振りをするだけですが、狂言で
は「エへ、エへ」と声を出しながら泣きます。

Q 狂言の装束にはどんな種類があるのでしょうか。

A 能に比べると狂言の装束は簡素な物が多
いようです。身分や性別によって着る物が決
定されています。大名は烏帽子という被り物
を付け、袴の裾を長く引いた裃を着ています。
太郎冠者などの身分の低い者は短めの袴をは
き、肩につけた肩衣には、鬼瓦やトンボなど
の虫が大きく描かれるなど意表を突いたデザ
インを施されているのが普通です。

肩衣

女性の役の場合、頭を白い長い布で覆い、
余った部分を耳から胸の方に垂らします。着
物は着流しで、腰を帯で締めます。歌舞伎の
女方のように女性らしい声を出すこともしま
せん。能楽師は白い足袋ですが、狂言師は黄
色い足袋をはきます。

Q 狂言では能のように面は付けないのでしょうか。

A 人間の場合には男役も女役も面を付けま
せんが、例外もあります。「釣針」などに出
てくるおもしろい顔をしている設定の女性
は、おかめのような「乙」の面を付け、高齢
の男性の場合も「祖父」という面を付けます。
　狂言で面を付けるものの大半は人間以外で

乙

the *shiori* gesture of placing one hand over the eyes, as if to hold back tears, but in kyōgen the character makes an *ehe, ehe* sound while crying.

Q What kinds of costumes are used in kyōgen?

Compared to nō, most kyōgen costumes are relatively plain. The clothing worn is determined by the character's social standing and gender. *Daimyō* wear *eboshi*-type headgear and the *kamishimo* style of formal attire, which includes long *hakama* (loose-fitting trousers). Characters of low social standing, such as Tarō Kaja, wear a shorter *hakama* and a *kataginu* (a type of vest) on which there is generally an uncommon design, such as a large picture of a gargoyle or an insect (dragonfly, etc.).

For female roles, the actor's head is covered with a long white cloth, the long ends of which hang down past the ears onto the chest. A kimono is worn with a sash tied around the hips. Unlike the *onnagata* (male actors in female roles) of kabuki, kyōgen actors do not try to use a feminine voice when they portray women. Nō actors wear white *tabi* (Japanese socks), whereas the *tabi* of kyōgen actors are yellow.

Q Are masks worn in kyōgen as they are in nō?

In kyōgen, human characters, whether male or female, do not wear masks. There are exceptions to this rule, however. In *Tsuribari* and other plays, the "funny-faced" female character wears an *oto* mask, which resembles the *okame* mask worn in folk plays. Actors playing old men sometimes wear the *ōji* mask.

Masks are used in kyōgen for non-human characters.

うそふき

す。狂言面は約20種類前後に分かれます。鬼の面、神様の面、巨大な蚊の精などに使うのが「うそふき」という口のとんがった面、男の幽霊の面、動物の「猿」「狐」「狸」などもあります。

　鬼や神様といっても能と違い、狂言面はどこか間が抜けていてユーモラスなのが特徴です。

Q 小道具や作り物にはどんなものがありますか。

扇

　A 重要なのが扇と葛桶です。扇は狂言方に限らず、シテ方、囃子方なども必携の物です。鋸や銚子や杯を表現する場合にも使いますし、主人が太郎冠者を招く場合、追う場合にも扇を使います。流儀により、図柄なども違い、役柄の地位などによって、地色も変わります。

葛桶

　葛桶も扇同様に、さまざまな物に変化します。腰掛けや酒樽、砂糖壺、水桶。そして「柿山伏」では山伏がよじ登る柿の木になり、「棒縛」では葛桶の蓋が盃になります。

　作り物は能と同様に竹などを使用した象徴的で、簡素なもので、能と同じ物を使う場合もあります。

There are about twenty different categories of kyōgen masks. The categories include *oni* (demon) masks, god masks, male spirit masks, animal masks (monkey, fox, *tanuki* [raccoon dog], etc.), and the *usofuki* mask, which has pursed lips and is used for, among other things, the spirit of a giant mosquito.

Unlike the masks used in nō, kyōgen masks, even those for gods and demons, have an offbeat and humorous aspect to them.

 ## Q What kinds of stage properties and set pieces are used in kyōgen?

The most important stage properties are the folding fans and the *kazuraoke*, a cylindrical, black-lacquer container.

Fans are carried not only by the kyōgen actors, but also by the nō *shite*, the musicians, etc. Fans are used to represent objects such as saké bottles, saké cups, and saws, and they are also used by the master both when beckoning Tarō Kaja and when chasing him. The different kyōgen schools have different designs on their fans, and the ground color varies depending on the status of the character.

Like a fan, a *kazuraoke* can be used to represent many things. It can become a water bucket, a saké cask, a sugar jar, or a stool to sit on. In *Kaki Yamabushi*, a *kazuraoke* becomes the *kaki* (persimmon) tree that the *yamabushi* (mountain ascetic) climbs. In *Bōshibari*, the lid of the *kazuraoke* becomes a saké cup.

The set pieces used on stage, usually made of bamboo and similar to those in nō, are simple and symbolic. Sometimes the same pieces are used in both nō and kyōgen.

文楽

Bunraku

文楽の誕生と発展

 一口に言って、文楽とはどんなものなのですか。

A 文楽は江戸時代に誕生した人形劇です。一般に「文楽」と言われるようになったのは明治以降のことで、昔は「人形浄瑠璃」と言われていました。

三味線の伴奏に乗せて「太夫」という語り手が物語を語り、それに合わせて舞台の上で人形遣いが人形を動かします。3者は一体です。

人形の動きは繊細で、時には人間以上に美しく、豪快に、悲しく物語を織り成して行きます。三味線の音色は体の芯に訴えるように、重く、美しいものです。

語り、三味線、人形——この3者が数百年の長きに亘り、それぞれの分野で工夫を加えた結果、文楽は世界でも指折りの高い芸術性を持つ人形劇に成長しました。

文楽の語りを「義太夫節」と言い、昭和の初期までは、これを趣味とする人がたくさんいました。有名な一節はほとんどの人が暗記しているほどでした。

文楽のために書かれた作品の多くは歌舞伎

ORIGINS AND HISTORY OF BUNRAKU

 In a word, what is bunraku?

Bunraku is the name of a form of puppet drama that arose during the Edo period (1600–1868). It was actually only during the Meiji period (1868–1912) that it started being called bunraku; before that, it was called *ningyō jōruri*, or puppet *jōruri*.

Bunraku is a union of three art forms in which a *tayū*, or narrator, narrates a story to musical accompaniment provided by a shamisen player, whilst on stage, doll manipulators make dolls perform to match the words of the *tayū*'s story.

The movements of the puppets are so delicate and subtle that at times the performances can be even more beautiful, exciting, and heart-rending than if human actors were being used. The shamisen provides music that is plaintive and evocative, capable of moving the audience to the core.

Each of the three elements that make up bunraku—narration, shamisen playing, and puppetry—underwent refinement in their own right over hundreds of years, the final result being the bunraku puppet drama we know today, one of the most highly sophisticated and artistic forms of puppet drama in the world.

The particular narration used in bunraku is called *gidayū-bushi* (*gidayū* narration), and until well into the beginning of the Shōwa period (1926–1989), many people in Japan made a hobby of learning how to sing this. At that time, almost everybody would know the most famous lines of plays by heart.

Most of the plays that were written for bunraku were also

にも取り入れられ、俳優のセリフや動きにも
影響を与えました。

 Q 文楽(人形浄瑠璃)はどのようにして
生まれてきたのですか。

A 日本には古来から英雄の物語を語って聞
かせる「語り物」という芸能がありました。
その語り物の1つとして、おそらく室町時代
(1333–1573)の末に生まれたと思われる物語
が、源義経の若き日である牛若丸と浄瑠璃姫
の恋を題材にした「浄瑠璃物語」でした。こ
の「浄瑠璃物語」が大流行した結果、節をつ
けて語るもの全体が「浄瑠璃」と言われるよ
うになってしまいました。

その後、浄瑠璃は、中国から渡ったと言わ
れる三味線を伴奏楽器として取り入れて発展
し、さらに、「人形操り」とも結びつきまし
た。

「人形操り」とは、文字どおり、人形を操る
見世物で、日本ではすでに平安時代ごろから、
各地を回り、道端で客を集め、人形を舞わせ
て金をもらう傀儡師と呼ばれる大道芸人がい
ました。当初はごく単純な動きだけをしてい
た人形も、時代を追うにしたがって仕掛けも
進歩し、複雑な動作をするようになりました。
この人形操りと浄瑠璃との結びつきによっ
て、江戸時代には人形浄瑠璃が完成されてい
ったのです。

傀儡師

performed on the kabuki stage. Bunraku also had an effect on actors' line delivery and movements.

Q What are the origins of bunraku (or *ningyō jōruri*)?

From ancient times in Japan, there existed the art of *katari-mono*, the telling of tales concerning the exploits of legendary figures. One such tale, *The Tale of Jōruri*, which was thought to have been written towards the end of the Muromachi period (1333–1573), was about the love of Minamoto Yoshitsune, known as Ushiwakamaru in his youth, and the Princess Jōruri. This tale became very popular, and eventually every kind of story narrated with a particular rhythm and intonation came to be referred to as a *jōruri*.

The art of *jōruri* then incorporated the musical accompaniment of the shamisen, said to have been brought over from China, after which further developments were made. The final addition occurred with the incorporation of *ningyō ayatsuri*.

Ningyō ayatsuri (doll manipulation) was the name for a kind of show that, just as the name implies, involved dolls, or puppets. It had existed as early as the Heian period (794–1185), when traveling performers, known as *kugutsu-shi* (doll players), traveled around the country performing dances with their dolls for payment. At first the dolls were only capable of performing the most rudimentary movements, but over the centuries their structure grew more sophisticated, and they eventually became capable of performing complicated actions and gestures. It was during the Edo period, when this *ningyō ayatsuri* joined up with *jōruri*, that *ningyō jōruri* was born.

浄瑠璃の語りを、なぜ「義太夫節」と呼ぶのですか。

A 義太夫とは、実は、人の名前なのです。江戸時代に、人形浄瑠璃は江戸、京都、大坂などに小屋(劇場)を構えて上演されました。大坂に登場した浄瑠璃の名手が竹本義太夫(1651–1714)です。

　義太夫は大坂に生まれ、先輩たちのもとで浄瑠璃の修業をした後に独立し、貞享元(1684)年に大坂に人形浄瑠璃を上演する竹本座を建てました。その旗揚げ興行で語った近松門左衛門作の「世継曾我」が成功を収め、翌年の近松による新作も観客に大歓迎されました。これによって義太夫の地位は確立され、彼の独特の節回しは「義太夫節」と言われるようになったのです。

文楽の作品と近松門左衛門

 義太夫とコンビを組んだ作者の近松門左衛門とはどんな人だったのですか。

近松門左衛門

A 近松(1653–1724)は、越前国(今の福井県)に武士の子として生まれました。父が浪人したため、一家は京都に上り、やがて近松は、人形浄瑠璃の脚本を書く仕事を始めたと言われています。

　彼が書いたことが確実視される最初の作品

Why is *jōruri* narration referred to
as *gidayū-bushi*?

The term *gidayū*, in fact, derives from the name of a person: the celebrated narrator Takemoto Gidayū (1651–1714), a man who came on the scene at a time during the Edo period when *ningyō jōruri* was still being performed in Edo, Kyōto, and Ōsaka in *koya*, or small playhouses.

Gidayū, a native of Ōsaka, decided to strike out on his own, once he had acquired a thorough training in *jōruri* under his elders. In Jōkyō 1 (1684), he established the Takemoto-za, a *ningyō jōruri* theater, in Ōsaka. The play he narrated to launch the theater was Chikamatsu Monzaemon's *Yotsugi Soga* (The Soga Heirs), which was very well received. The following year, a new work by Chikamatsu also met with a highly enthusiastic reception from its audiences. *Gidayū*'s position as the leading narrator of his day was thus assured, and thereafter his unique method of intoning the narration came to be referred to as *gidayū-bushi* (*gidayū* narration).

THE PLAYS OF BUNRAKU AND CHIKAMATSU MONZAEMON

 What is known about Chikamatsu Monzaemon, the playwright who teamed up with *gidayū*?

Chikamatsu (1653–1724) was born into a samurai family in Echizen (present-day Fukui Prefecture). When his father became masterless, however, the whole family moved to Kyōto, which is where, the story goes, Chikamatsu eventually took work writing scripts for *ningyō jōruri* plays.

The first verfied work by Chikamatsu that established his

が竹本義太夫の語った「世継曾我」です。以降、近松は続け様に浄瑠璃作品を発表し、押しも押されもしない人気作者となりました。

それまでは人形浄瑠璃では、語りをする「太夫」が一番重んじられ、浄瑠璃作者は太夫に従属する一段低い地位の者と考えられていました。しかし、近松が人気作者となったことで作者の地位も向上しました。

歌舞伎界でも彼の才能は注目されました。当時人気の歌舞伎俳優、坂田藤十郎とは元禄6(1693)年から約10年間もコンビを組み、藤十郎のためにいくつもの狂言を書きました。その間は近松は主に歌舞伎狂言作者として活躍したわけです。しかし、彼は元禄16(1703)年に発表した「曾根崎心中」で、再び浄瑠璃作者として注目を集めます。

歌舞伎は役者本位となりがちで、人形浄瑠璃のように物語を重視した台本が書きにくかったことが、近松が人形浄瑠璃界に戻った大きな原因と言われています。

Q どうして「曾根崎心中」という作品は、世間の注目を集めたのですか。

A 人形浄瑠璃の作品としては、初めて、町人の社会の出来事や人物に取材したものだったからです。

それまでの浄瑠璃のほとんどは、歴史上の

reputation was *Yotsugi Soga* (*The Soga Heirs*), which Takemoto Gidayū narrated. After this success, Chikamatsu went on to produce a steady stream of *jōruri* plays, and he soon became one of the most successful and highly acclaimed playwrights of his day.

Until Chikamatsu's time, the person accorded primary importance in *ningyō jōruri* had always been the *tayū*, or narrator. The playwright occupied a position that was secondary and subservient to the *tayū*. After Chikamatsu achieved such recognition, however, the status of playwrights rose accordingly.

Chikamatsu's superb ability as a playwright also gained him attention in the world of kabuki. In Genroku 6 (1693), he teamed up with the popular kabuki actor Sakata Tōjūro and, over a period of roughly ten years, wrote a number of plays especially for him. But in Genroku 16 (1703), with his masterpiece *Sonezaki Shinjū* (Love Suicides at Sonezaki), he once again started to get attention as a playwright of *jōruri* plays.

The reason for Chikamatsu's return to *jōruri* is thought to have its root in the fact that whereas in kabuki the actors are considered paramount, in *ningyō jōruri* it is the story that matters most, thus allowing the writer greater exercise of his powers.

 Why did the play *Sonezaki Shinjū* (Love Suicides at Sonezaki) become such a hit with its audiences?

Because this was the first time that a *ningyō jōruri* piece had taken as its subject the lives of ordinary people in Edo-period merchant society.

Previously, most *jōruri* plays had consisted of *jidaimono*,

偉い人物や有名な事件を題材にした「時代物」でした。それに対し「曾根崎心中」の主人公は、醬油屋の使用人である徳兵衛と遊女のお初です。

近松は上演の1ヵ月前に大坂で実際にあった事件を題材にして、この2人が曾根崎の森で心中するまでのいきさつを描きました。2人が心中場所の森へたどりつくまでの道中を描いた「道行」の文章は特に名文として知られています。

曾根崎心中

庶民の娯楽の人形浄瑠璃に初めて庶民を主人公にした作品が生まれたわけです。実際にあった事件を劇化したことで、今で言えば週刊誌的な興味も満足させられ、「曾根崎心中」は大当たりとなりました。

Q 近松はほかにどんな浄瑠璃を書いていますか。

A 近松はなかなか多作家で、24編の世話物と70編の時代物を残しています。

町人の社会を舞台にした世話物には「心中天網島」「冥途の飛脚」「堀川波鼓」「女殺油地獄」などがあります。実際の事件に題材を得た心中や人殺し、敵討ちなどの話がほとんどです。

曾根崎心中

historical plays about famous figures and incidents. The protagonists of *Sonezaki Shinjū*, in contrast, were an ordinary employee at a soy sauce store, Tokubee, and a prostitute, O-Hatsu.

Basing his play on an incident that had actually happened in Ōsaka just one month before the production, Chikamatsu focused on the developments that led up to two lovers committing love suicide together in the forest at Sonezaki. The lines describing the journey the two lovers make to the woods where they kill themselves are particularly well known, and are amongst the most famous passages in the entire *jōruri* repertoire.

For all that it was an entertainment for ordinary people, *ningyō jōruri* had never before featured ordinary folk in its starring roles. The fact that this play dramatized an incident that had actually occurred gave it an extra, sensational interest, all of which led to *Sonezaki Shinjū* becoming a major success.

 Q **What other *jōruri* plays did Chikamatsu write?**

Chikamatsu was an extremely prolific playwright. He wrote twenty-four *sewamono* (plays about ordinary Edo townspeople) and seventy *jidaimono* (historical plays).

Amongst his *sewamono* are such pieces as *Shinjū Ten no Amishima* (Love Suicides at Ten no Amishima), *Meido no Hikyaku* (The Courier for Hell), *Horikawa Nami no Tsuzumi*, (The Drum in the Waves of Horikawa), *Onna-Goroshi Abura no Jigoku*. Chikamatsu's *sewamono* nearly all concern lovers' suicides, murders, or vendettas, and are based on incidents that happened in real life.

　歴史上の事件や人物を扱った時代物には、平清盛に反乱を企てて失敗し、島に流された「俊寛」で有名な「平家女護島」や、日本人と中国人の間に生まれた和唐内を主人公に中国を舞台にした「国性爺合戦」、絵師の又平を主人公にした「傾城反魂香」などがあります。

Q 近松の後は、人形浄瑠璃作者の世界はどのように変わって行きましたか。

　A　「曾根崎心中」のヒットした元禄16（1703）年に、義太夫の弟子の豊竹若太夫が新しい劇場の豊竹座を興しましたが、この豊竹座では紀海音（1663–1742）という作者を起用し、海音も人気作者となりました。

　近松と海音が競い合うように作品を書き、また2つの劇場はことごとに張り合い、語り口などに特色を持たせたため、人形浄瑠璃はますます隆盛となりました。竹本座は地味でしっとりとし、豊竹座は華やかな芸風だったと言われています。

　竹本座が大坂の道頓堀の西側にあったため、その芸風を「西風」、対して豊竹座は東にあったため、その芸風を「東風」と言います。この西風、東風という言い方は現在の文楽でも生きています。

　近松、海音以降の浄瑠璃は大きく変わって

Amongst Chikamatsu's *jidaimono* are pieces such as the celebrated play *Heike Nyogogashima*, otherwise known as *Shunkan*, about the nobleman who plotted to overthrow Taira no Kiyomori and was exiled to an island as punishment; *Kokusenya Kassen* (The Battles of Kokusenya), set in China, about *kokusenya*, a man of mixed heritage called Watonai, born to a Japanese man and a Chinese woman; and *Keisei Hangonkō*, a play about an artist named Matahei.

 What developments took place in *ningyō jōruri* theater after Chikamatsu?

In the same year that *Sonezaki Shinjū* became a smash hit, Gidayū's disciple Toyotake Wakadayū set up a new theater, the Toyotake-za. Here he appointed as theater director the playwright Ki no Kaion (1663–1742), who also became highly successful.

Chikamatsu and Kaion thereafter competed with each other in writing plays, and the two theaters also tried to outdo each other in any way they could by, for example, developing unique flavor and characteristics in the narration. Thanks to this rivalry, *ningyō jōruri* went on to enjoy a period of great prosperity. The style of the Takemoto-za was held to be somber and restrained, while that of the Toyotake-za was lavish and showy.

The Takemoto-za was situated on the west bank of Ōsaka's Dōtombori, which led to its particular style being called the West Style. The Toyotake-za was situated on the east bank, which led to its style being dubbed the East Style. These two terms are still current in present-day bunraku.

After Chikamatsu and Kaion's time, some significant

行きます。1つは、1人の作者が全編を書く形式から数人の作者が合作するようになったこと。そしてもう1つは、人形の遣い方の変化です。

浄瑠璃の時代物は「段」と呼ばれる物語の部分から構成されています。時代物はおおむね5段形式ですが、これを何人かで合作するようになりました。この場合、中心になる作者を特に立作者と言います。

仮名手本忠臣蔵

文楽には3大名作と呼ばれる人気作品があります。「仮名手本忠臣蔵」「菅原伝授手習鑑」「義経千本桜」がそうですが、この3作品も並木千柳、三好松洛、竹田出雲という3人の作者によって合作されたものです。

物語の構成と表現の特徴

 文楽の作品の構成はどうなっているのでしょう。

A 上演演目は、歴史上の出来事や人物をテーマとした「時代物」と、町人社会の事件や人物をテーマとした「世話物」に分けられます。

時代物は5つの部分からなる5段構成が基本

changes took place in *jōruri*. One change concerned the playwright: from this time on, instead of one playwright being responsible for the script from beginning to end, it became a joint production, the work of several playwrights. Another change was in the way the puppets were manipulated.

Jōruri jidaimono (historical plays) are composed of different sections or acts, known as *dan*. The majority of *jidaimono* are comprised of five *dan*, and several people would have a hand in writing them. In such circumstances, the main playwright had a specific designation as the *tate sakusha*, or principal writer.

There are three works in bunraku, referred to as the *San Daimeisaku*, or Big Three, that remain the most well-known and popular: *Kanadehon Chūshingura* (The Treasury of Loyal Retainers), *Sugawara Denju Tenarai Kagami* (The Secret of Sugawara's Calligraphy), and *Yoshitsune Sembonzakura* (The Thousand Cherry Trees). These plays were all the combined works of three playwrights, Namiki Senryū, Miyoshi Shūraku, and Takeda Izumo.

PLOT LINE AND FEATURES OF PRESENTATION

 What can you tell me about the composition of bunraku plays?

Plays in the bunraku repertoire can be divided into two categories: *jidaimono*, which deal with historical events and persons, and *sewamono*, which deal with events and people in Edo society.

The standard *jidaimono* usually consists of five *dan*, or

です。初段（1段目）では事件の発端が描かれ、2段目では、主人公たちが事件によって窮地に陥り、3段目では悲劇が決定的となります。4段目で解決の糸口が見つかり、5段目で万事めでたく治まるという構成です。

「世話物」は普通は上中下の3巻で構成されています。

各々の段は「端場」あるいは「口」と言われる導入部分と、クライマックスになる「切場」で構成されています。

「端場」は通常、若手の太夫と三味線が受け持ちます。重要な場面である「切場」は、実力のある太夫と三味線弾きが受け持つ場合が多く、そうした太夫は「切場語りの太夫」と尊敬を込めて呼ばれます。「切場語り」は演目や出演者の名前などを書いた「番付」の名の上に「切」と書くことを許されます。

 文楽の演目には、歌舞伎のような舞踊はないのでしょうか。

A あります。文楽ではこの踊りの場面を、「景事」とも「道行」ともいいます。

「道行」は歌舞伎の用語にもなっていますが、ある場所からほかの場所へ旅することを指します。その間の変わり行く景色や風物などをつづり、旅の情緒を出します。義太夫節では「道行」を入れるのが決まりのようになっていて、時代物では「四段目」の「口」に、世

acts. The first act depicts the lead-up to the incident; the second, how the protagonists are caught in a difficult situation; and the third, how the tragedy comes to a head. In the fourth, a possible way out of the dilemma becomes evident; and in the fifth act, events come to an end on a suitably propitious note.

Sewamono are usually composed of three *maki* (literally, volumes), divided into *jō*, *chū*, and *ge* (first, middle, and last).

Each *dan*, or act, is composed of its own introductory section, referred to as the *haba* (verge) or *kuchi* (mouth), followed by a climactic scene, referred to as the *kiriba* (cutting scene).

During the introductory scenes, a less experienced *tayū* and shamisen player usually provide the narration and musical accompaniment. In the climactic scenes, however, which are the most important, it is common for a highly experienced *tayū* and shamisen player to take over. Such master *tayū* are given the respectful designation *kiribagatari no tayū*, or cutting-scene *tayū*. These experienced narrators are listed on the *banzuke* (play programs), with the character for "cut" printed above their names.

Does bunraku feature dance, like kabuki?

In bunraku, the dance interludes occur in places known both as *kei-goto* (scene things) and *michiyuki* (travel dances).

The term *michiyuki*, also used in kabuki, refers to that section of the play where the protagonists make a journey, leaving one place to go to another. One by one, the views and places of note that the protagonists pass through on their travels are woven into the narration to evoke the mood and ambiance of a journey. In *gidayū-bushi*, such *michiyuki* scenes have become

話物では下の巻に置かれました。

「義経千本桜」の「吉野山」などがそれに当たります。「吉野山」は狐の化身である忠信と義経の恋人、静御前の主従が義経の元へと旅をする様をつづったものです。

義経千本桜

　近松の場合は、「世話物」の「道行」は恋する男女が一緒に死ぬ、心中までの旅路という傾向が強いようです。「曾根崎心中」の「道行」や、「心中天網島」の橋の名を読み込んだ「橋づくし」などが有名です。

Q 文楽の作品には悲劇が多いと聞いていますが、事実でしょうか。

　A 確かに文楽の多くは悲劇作品です。悲劇のほうが喜劇よりは、大きな物語を作りやすいのが原因の1つでしょうし、扱っている題材が戦争やお家騒動に心中であれば、どうしても悲劇的になります。

　その中に滑稽な役柄や場面が出てくる場合があり、これを「チャリ」と言います。どんなにうまくできた悲劇でもそればかり見せられていては観客も疲れます。そこでちょっとした息抜きの場面として作られたのが「チャリ」です。

　「チャリ」には、大きく分けて、一場面が全て滑稽な場合と、悲劇の中にチャリの役が出

a standard item: in *jidaimono* plays, they occur at the start of the fourth *dan*; and in *sewamono* plays, in the final *maki*.

An example of the latter comes in the *Yoshino Yama* (Yoshino Mountains) passage in *Yoshitsune Sembon Zakura*. The *michiyuki* here weaves in the place names of the journey to Yoshitsune's camp made by two people, the retainer Tadanobu, who is really a fox in disguise, and the noblewoman Shizuka Gozen, who is Yoshitsune's lover.

In Chikamatsu's case, the *michiyuki* in his *sewamono* plays nearly always feature a man and a woman who are lovers finding their way to a place where they will commit suicide together. His most celebrated *michiyuki* include the one in *Sonezaki Shinjū*, and the one in *Shinjū Ten no Amejima*, where the names of bridges are woven into the narration.

Q **Would it be correct to say that the majority of bunraku plays are tragedies?**

Certainly, most bunraku plays are tragedies. One reason for this is probably that it is easier to write an epic story for a tragedy than for a comedy. Since most of the material for the plots tends to center on battles and family disputes, inevitably, the plays do take on a tragic cast.

But there are places where comic characters appear and comic situations develop. These are referred to as *chari* (comical scenes or scenes of buffoonery). Even the most masterful of tragic plays would be oppressive for the audience if it were completely unremitting, and this is where these *chari* scenes come in handy, providing a brief respite.

There are two categories of *chari*: the kind where an entire scene will consist of a comic situation and the kind where a

チャリ

てくるものとの2種類あります。

「桂川連理柵」という作品は、年の離れた男女の心中を扱った悲劇です。よく上演されるのは「帯屋」という場面ですが、ここにも丁稚の長吉という「チャリ」役が登場します。「チャリ」役の、何も分からない無神経な言動が、主人公たちの悲しみを一層観客に印象づける効果も生みます。

Q 文楽で言う「物語」とはどういうことなのでしょうか。

A 「物語」といってもストーリーのことではありません。「物」を「語る」ことから出た言葉です。時代物の立役の主人公が、過去の自分も関わった重要な事件について周囲の人々に語り聞かせることをさします。

「一谷嫩軍記」の「熊谷陣屋」や、「源平布引滝」の「実盛物語」の「物語」など、多くの作品がこの「物語」のシーンを見せ場としています。

「熊谷陣屋」で物語るのは熊谷直実です。作品全体の背景は源氏と平家の争いで、すでに平家の敗色が濃く、一門は次々と命を落としています。この前の「檀特山」という場面で、熊谷は平家の平敦盛を討って命を奪ったことになっています。

敦盛の母の藤の方は、息子を心配して熊谷

comic character will come on in the midst of a tragic situation.

A comic scene occurs in the play *Katsuragawa Renri no Shigarami*, a tragedy about the love suicide of a man and woman of widely differing ages. This scene, known as the Obi Shop scene, a particular favorite, is often performed. In it, Chōkichi, a shop boy, has the comic role. If anything, these comic characters and their foolish, innocent words and actions have the effect of making the plight of the protagonists even more deeply moving for the audience.

 Q **What can you tell me about *monogatari* in bunraku?**

The term *monogatari* signifies much more than "story." The word actually derives from two words: *kataru* (telling) of *mono* (a thing). In bunraku, the word *monogatari* refers to the tale that a principal character will relate to others about an important event in the past in which he himself was involved.

In many bunraku pieces, the *monogatari* scene forms the highlight of the play. Such *monogatari* scenes would include the Kumagai's Camp scene in *Ichinotani Futaba Gunki* (The Chronicle of the Battle of Ichinotani), and Sanemori's Story in *Genpei Nunobiki no Taki*.

In Kumagai's Camp, the person who tells the *monogatari* is Kumagai Naozane. The wars between the Heike and the Genji clans form a backdrop to the whole play and, by this point, the prospects for a Heike defeat look certain. One by one, the warriors in the Heike family are being slain. In the previous scene, known as Dantokusen, the Genji warrior Kumagai has slain the young Heike warrior Atsumori.

Atsumori's mother, Fuji no Kata, visits Kumagai's quar-

の陣屋を訪ねました。やはり出陣した子供の小次郎を気遣って熊谷の妻の相模も陣屋に来ています。相模はその昔、藤の方に仕えていました。2人が熊谷が敦盛を討ったという噂を聞き、案じているところへ熊谷が帰還します。隠れていた藤の方は、敦盛を殺したのは本当だという熊谷の言葉を聞いて、切り掛かります。熊谷は藤の方を制して、敦盛を討った経緯を語ります。それが「物語」です。

　熊谷の人形は正面を向いて扇を構えて物語を始めます。自分自身のことはもちろん、敦盛の動きやセリフ、それに一騎打ちの行われた海辺での様子など周囲の状況までをも、熊谷は物語の中で表現します。実際は、熊谷ではなく、語るのは太夫であり、動くのは人形ですが、観客はそれを熊谷が1人で過去の事件を語ることとして見聞きします。

　太夫の語りも三味線も人形も、現在、戦いが行われているかのごとく、語り、弾き、動きます。熊谷が語るところでは勇ましく、敦盛の台詞のところは優しく語り、それに合わせて人形も動いていきます。「檀特山」の場面をみた観客は、自分で見たものを、今度は、熊谷の語りとして再体験するわけです。

ters, fearing for her son. Kumagai's wife, Sagami, is there too, worried about her own son, Kojirō, who is also out on the battlefield. Many years ago, Sagami was a lady-in-waiting in the service of Fuji no Kata. Just as the two women hear rumors that Kumagai has slain Atsumori and wonder anxiously whether they might be true, Kumagai returns to camp. Fuji no Kata listens from a hiding place as Kumagai confirms that the rumors are true: she then attacks Kumagai with a sword. But Kumagai restrains her, and proceeds to give an account of how he brought Atsumori down. This account is the *monogatari*.

Facing the audience, holding his fan straight out in front of him, Kumagai commences his tale. During the tale, he of course enacts his own thoughts and state of mind at the time, but he will also evoke the movements and words of his opponent Atsumori, as well as describing the stretch of shore where the two men engaged in single-handed combat and the atmosphere of the scene. Of course, realistically speaking, the *tayū* is relating the words, and the doll simply miming the movements. But as the audience listens, it will seem as if it is truly Kumagai who is relating the story all by himself.

As the *tayū*, shamisen player, and puppeteers all put their utmost into their performance, the combat seems to take place before the audience's eyes. Kumagai's own words and actions are narrated in a tone of manly vigor, but when Atsumori speaks, his tone becomes soft and the doll's movements are modulated accordingly. The audience, who has already seen Atsumori's death in the previous scene, will experience it here a second time, in Kumagai's narration.

女形には「口説」という特有の表現のしかたが
あるそうですが、どんな表現ですか。

A 女形の人形が、嘆き悲しむ場面で用いる、切々たる物語りが「口説」です。切ない胸の内を表現する語りに合わせて人形は全身で悲しみを描き出します。

「艶容女舞衣」の「酒屋」の場で、夫に捨てられたお園が、「今頃は半七っつぁん」と言う場面などは、昭和の前半までがだれもが知っている「口説」の場面でした。

先程の「熊谷陣屋」では相模の「口説」があります。「熊谷陣屋」では熊谷が討った敦盛は実は熊谷の子の小次郎だったことが明らかとなります。それを知った母の相模は、熊谷や藤の方を前に、小次郎を失った悲しみを訴えます。この「口説」の間は周囲の人形はじっとしていて動きません。観客の目は相模のみにそそがれます。

Q 「もどり」という手法も文楽でよく使われるそうですが、どんな手法ですか。

A 悪人と思われていた人間が、善人である本性を見せるのが「もどり」です。「摂州合邦辻」という作品の「合邦庵室」の段の玉手御前の「もどり」の場を例にとってみましょう。

Q There is a special method used in the performance of puppets in female roles, known as *kudoki*. What does *kudoki* involve?

Kudoki refers to the deeply affecting and mournful narration used in scenes when dolls in female roles express grief and lamentation. In these scenes, the doll is manipulated to make her entire body exude sadness, to match the heart-rending emotions being narrated.

These *kudoki* scenes were familiar to almost everybody up until the 1950s. For example, one very well-known *kudoki* scene was the Saké Shop scene in *Hadesugata Onna no Maiginu*, where O-Sono, abandoned by her husband, pours out her sadness in a plaintive passage that begins: "Oh, this time last year, Hanshichi …"

Another *kudoki* scene occurs in the Kumagai's Camp scene, for Sagami. It becomes clear in Kumagai's Camp that the young man whom Kumagai slew was not actually Atsumori but his own son, Kojiro. When this becomes known to Sagami, she expresses her grief at the loss of her son to Kumagai and Fuji no Kata. During this narration, the dolls around Sagami remain quite motionless, frozen, allowing the audience's attention to focus solely on her.

Q What is involved in *modori*, another bunraku convention?

Modori (return, recovery) is the term used to refer to what happens when a character who has seemed all along to be a villain shows through some speech or action that he or she is in fact a person of virtue. One such example occurs for Tamate Gozen in *Sesshū Gappō ga Tsuji*, in the scene known as Gappō's Hermitage.

玉手御前は大名家の後妻ですが、義理の息子の俊徳丸に恋をして、顔の崩れる毒酒を飲ませて、婚約者のいる彼を独り占めにしようとします。体の弱った俊徳丸は、婚約者の浅香姫と一緒に、玉手の父である合邦の家に匿われています。玉手は俊徳丸を探して実家を訪れ、自分がいかに俊徳丸を好きかを訴え、怒った合邦に刺されてしまいます。死に瀕した玉手は善人に戻り、俊徳丸に毒を飲ませたのは、お家騒動から彼を守るためだったのだと、切々と真実、本心を語ります。これが「もどり」です。

「義経千本桜」の「すし屋」のいがみの権太、「菅原伝授手習鑑」の「寺子屋」の松王丸などの「もどり」の場も有名です。

菅原伝授手習鏡

現代演劇とは違い、玉手も権太も松王丸も「もどり」になるまでは、実は善人だということをほのめかしたりはしません。「もどり」まではあくまでも憎々しく、嫌な人間としての芝居をします。

義太夫節と三味線

 太夫は文楽の中ではどんな役割を果たすのですか。

A 文楽は義太夫を語る太夫、三味線弾き、人形遣いの3者が力を合わせることで成立し

In this play, Tamate Gozen, the second wife of a *daimyō*, falls in love with her stepson Shuntokumaru. In the hope of preventing him from marrying his fiancée, she makes him drink poison, which ruins his good looks. In a much weakened state, Shuntokumaru takes refuge with his lover Asaka in the household of Gappō, Tamate's father. Tamate visits her father's dwelling looking for Shuntokumaru. When she tries to explain her passion for the young man, Gappō loses his temper, and stabs her. As she dies, Tamate "recovers" and shows that she is a person of virtue: she proceeds to relate her true feelings, and the truth of the situation—that the real reason she made Shuntokumaru drink poison was to save him from family scandal. This is the kind of sudden change for the good that *modori* refers to.

Other celebrated *modori* occur for Igami no Gonta in *Yoshitsune Sembon Zakura*, in the Sushi Shop scene, and for Matsuomaru in *Sugawara Denju Tenarai Kagami*, in the Village School scene.

These *modori* completely disregard psychological consistency, something that a modern audience might find strange. None of the characters to whom these *modori* occur shows any sign beforehand that he or she has any virtue: they are all simply depicted as the most detestable characters imaginable.

GIDAYŪ NARRATION AND SHAMISEN ACCOMPANIMENT

 How important is the *tayū* in bunraku?

Bunraku comes into being with the joint effort of three groups: the *tayū*, who chants the narration; the shamisen play-

太夫と三味線弾き

ています。この3者のことを「三業」といいます。三業が一体となって1つの芸術を作り出すわけですが、中でも、全体をリードするのが太夫です。

太夫と三味線弾きは舞台の上手（右側）にある高座（これを床と言います）に座って、語りと伴奏を行います。床は回転するようになっていて、その場面を担当する太夫と三味線弾きは、2人一緒に床に乗って、屏風の後ろからぐるっと回って観客の前へ登場します。舞台に近い、左側に太夫、右側に三味線弾きが座ります。

太夫は語っている間に、舞台の人形の動きを見るようなことはしません。前の見台に台本（文楽では「床本」と言います）を置いて、これを見ながら、自分自身の解釈で語ります。床本には太夫が語る文章と、朱と呼ばれる音符代わりの記号などが書き込まれています。床本は、太夫が自分自身で手書きするのが普通です。

太夫は1人で複数の人物を語り分けます。男性も、女性も、老人も、子供も、1人で語っていくわけです。それだけではありません。登場人物の喜怒哀楽から、天候や季節、都会か田舎かなどの状況や情景までを観客に伝えなければなりません。太夫は重大な役割を担っているのです。

er, who provides the musical accompaniment; and the puppeteers, who move the dolls. These three spheres, narration, shamisen playing, and puppetry, are referred to as *san gyō* (the three arts). But even though all three are vital to bunraku, nevertheless, the *tayū*, or narrator, holds paramount importance.

The *tayū* is seated with the shamisen player on the *yuka* (a raised dais) to the right of the stage, where the narration and musical accompaniment take place. This dais is in fact built in such a way that it can rotate, so that when the time comes for a new pair of *tayū* and shamisen player to come on, they take their places in readiness behind the painted screen on the dais, which then swings around to bring them out in front. The *tayū* is seated nearest the audience, while the shamisen player is seated on the *tayū*'s right-hand side.

The *tayū* never looks over at the stage to see what the puppets are doing while he is narrating. He simply concentrates on rendering his own particular interpretation of the lines, reading from the script (referred to in bunraku as the *yukahon*), which is placed on a small rest in front of him. The pages of the script are inscribed with the words of the lines he has to narrate, as well as various markings and symbols, known as *shu*, which are comparable to musical notation. It is usual for the *tayū* to narrate from a copy of the play that he has written out for himself.

During the play, the *tayū* has single-handedly to narrate all sorts of different parts—men and women, old people and children. And that is not all: aside from the plethora of moods and emotions in the characters themselves, he also has to describe the weather and the particular season the action takes place in, as well as aspects of the locality and the scenery. A great deal of responsibility rests on his shoulders.

　初めて文楽を見た人は、顔を真っ赤にして出す太夫の大声に驚かされたことと思います。それに、太夫のお腹が前に張り出しているので、随分太っているなあと、不思議に思われるかもしれません。

　義太夫節は腹式呼吸で声を出すのですが、声を出しやすくするために、お腹には「腹帯」という幅10センチほどの布を巻き、そこに「おとし」と呼ばれる砂ぶくろを入れています。重心を下に置くことで、腹がしっかりとし、声がよく出るようになるわけです。このためにお腹がでているように見えるわけです。

　肩には「肩衣」を付け、袴をはきます。床本を乗せた見台を前に、「尻敷」という小さな台の上にお尻を乗せて座ります。語り始める前に、太夫は義太夫節への敬意を込めて床本を押し戴きます。

Q 義太夫節はどんな構成になっているのですか。

　A 大きく分けて「地合」「詞」「フシ」の3つから構成されています。

「地合」は「地」とも言いますが、状況や情景の説明をする部分です。小説で言えば、会話以外の部分、脚本で言えば、ト書きの部分と言っていいでしょう。朗読風のものと、歌うような旋律風のものとがあります。

　詞とは登場人物の話すセリフのことです。

People seeing bunraku for the first time are no doubt amazed by the sight of the *tayū* getting red in the face, putting every ounce of energy and concentration into his narration. No doubt they are also surprised by how portly he looks.

There is a reason for the tayu's protruding belly. In *gidayū-bushi*, the *tayū* narrates taking deep breaths from the stomach. In order to facilitate this, a *haraobi* (wide band of cloth) is wrapped around his belly, which holds in place a small sandbag, known as an *otoshi*. This helps lower the center of gravity in the body and support the stomach, as well, so that the *tayū*'s voice can come out loud and clear.

The *tayū* wears a *kataginu* (sleeveless ceremonial robe), over his kimono, and *hakama* (ceremonial trousers). With the script rest placed before him, he will be seated on a small dais. Before the *tayū* commences his narration, he will raise the script reverently to his head in a gesture of respect.

Q What are the different elements in *gidayū-bushi*?

Basically speaking, *gidayū-bushi* (*gidayū* narration) is comprised of three elements: *jiai*, *kotoba* and *fushi*.

Jiai, also known as *ji*, refers to those parts of the narration that provide descriptions of circumstances or scenery. In a novel, *jiai* would be comparable to any prose that is not conversation; in a playbook, it would be comparable to the stage directions. There are two different kinds of *jiai*: *jiai* that is spoken as if it were being read and the *jiai* that is modulated as if it were being sung.

Kotoba refers to the conversations and lines spoken by the

詞が語られている間は三味線の伴奏はありません。

フシはメロディーです。詞が一段落して地合に移る間の旋律です。

Q 太夫はいつも1人で語るのでしょうか。

A 太夫は1人で語るのが原則ですが、時には、「掛合」と言って、数人の太夫でそれぞれの役を受け持つ場合もあります。近松半二の代表作「妹背山婦女庭訓」の「山の段」を例にしてみましょう。「山の段」には対立する家の娘と息子の恋が描かれており、シェイクスピアの「ロミオとジュリエット」とよく比較されます。

舞台の上には上手の背山に大判事の館、下手の妹山に定高という女性の館があります。大判事の息子の久我之助と定高の娘の雛鳥は恋仲です。

この場面では上手だけでなく、下手にも床が設けられ、初演の時には、情を語る名人と言われた竹本染太夫が背山を、美声で有名だった竹本春太夫が妹山を掛け合いで語り、大評判となりました。その形式が現在にまで引き継がれ、大判事、久我之助、定高、雛鳥をそれぞれ1人の太夫が語るようになっています。

characters in the play. During such *kotoba* narration, the shamisen remains completely silent.

Fushi means "melody," and simply refers to the music played in the pauses after *kotoba*, before the narration shifts back to *jiai*.

Q Does the *tayū* always narrate single-handedly?

The *tayū*, in principle, narrates alone. However, there are rare occasions when several *tayū* narrate, in what is known as a *kake-ai* (dialogue or cross-calling). *Kake-ai* is used, for example, in a famous passage known as the Mountains scene in Chikamatsu Hanji's celebrated play *Imoseyama Onna Teikin* (An Example of Noble Womanhood). This play features the love between the daughter and son of two feuding families —an aspect which has led to the play being compared to Shakespeare's *Romeo and Juliet*.

The stage is set with two country palaces, one on either side: on the right, a residence in Seyama that belongs to the lord Daihanji; and on the left, a residence in Imoyama that belongs to the lady Sadaka. The fated lovers are Daihanji's son Koganosuke and Sadaka's daughter Hinadori.

In the Mountains scene, two dais are set up, on both the right and left of the stage. In the first production, Takemoto Sometayū, celebrated for his emotional renditions, narrated the Seyama side, and Takemoto Harutayū, who was famed for his extraordinarily beautiful voice, answered for the Imoyama side. The play created a sensation. The format continues to be favored to the present day, with Daihanji and Koganosuke, and Sadaka and Hinadori each being narrated by their own *tayū*.

太夫はどんな声の出し方で表現をしていくのですか。

A 太夫は、声の高低や息の出し方、抑揚の微妙な使い分けなどで、それぞれの人物や心理を描き出していきます。しかし、太夫は1人で何役もこなすため、俳優と違って、「役になりきってはいけない」といわれます。なりきる一歩手前で止めておかないと、次の人物にすぐ変わることができないからです。

基本的には、時代物で、勇ましい英雄や武将が主人公のときは、声量豊かに、豪快に、ゆったりと語ります。それに対して、世話物の主人公のときは、明るく、テンポよく、写実的に語ります。

悲しみの表現で用いるのが「落し」という方法です。今まで語っていた音程を一段と下げたり、声を抑えたりします。最も激しいのが「大落し」で、時代物でのみ使われます。

「妹背山婦女庭訓」の「山の段」で、雛鳥の母である定高と久我之助の父の大判事が、互いの子の死を知り、吉野川を挟んで悲嘆にくれる場面での悲しみの表現に「大落し」が使われています。

また、「絵本太功記」の「尼ヶ崎」で武智

Q What are the ways in which the *tayū* will use his voice in his narration?

The *tayū* has a variety of ways in which to evoke the character and psychology of the characters in the play he narrates. He can modulate the volume of his voice, he can draw his breath and let it out in various ways, he can subtly vary the rhythm and cadence of his narration. But since he has to handle numerous characters all by himself, unlike an actor, he must stop short of identifying completely with any particular person, because always in the next moment he will have to become somebody else.

As a rule, in *jidaimono* (historical plays), where brave-hearted heroes and generals are the protagonists, the *tayū* narrates in a dignified, stirring and stately way. In contrast, in *sewamono* (plays about ordinary people), the narration is conducted in a bright, fast-moving, realistic way.

There is one particular method where the voice is "dropped," known as *otoshi*, used in moments when the *tayū* is rendering a character's grief. At these points the *tayū* takes the register at which he has been narrating one grade lower and proceeds in a voice that denotes barely restrained emotion. In extremely tragic scenes, the method of narrating is known as *ō-otoshi*. This is used only in *jidaimono*.

In the Mountains scene in *Imoseyama Onna Teikin*, there is a famous section where Hinadori's mother, Sadaka, and Koganosuke's father, Daihanji, discover that their children have died, and they give themselves over to grief, on opposite sides of the Yoshino River. This is one scene where *ō-otoshi* narration is used.

Another *ō-otoshi* scene occurs in *Ehon Taikōki* (The

光秀が、母の皐月と息子の十次郎の死を目の前にして大泣きするのも「大落し」です。

　太夫が大きな声で情感を込めて語るときは、三味線も大変です。「タタキバチ」と言い、絃を弾くだけではなく、三味線の皮にバチを叩き付けるようにして音を出します。

 Q 義太夫の「笑い」はとても印象的ですが、どんな特徴があるのでしょうか。

　A 太夫が顔を真っ赤にして、声を限りに続ける文楽の笑いは、観客に強い印象を残すものの1つです。

　有名な笑いがいくつもあります。例えば「菅原伝授手習鑑」の敵役である藤原時平の笑いです。この狂言は高潔な菅原道真が、時平の企みで、官職を奪われたことによって巻き起こる悲劇が描かれています。

　その時平は「車引」の場面で、道真たちに忠義立てをする梅王丸、桜丸らを「うじ虫め」とあざ笑います。この時の時平の笑い。

　そして「仮名手本忠臣蔵」の高師直の笑い。「三段目」で師直は塩冶判官をさんざん馬鹿にして、世間知らずの「鮒」のようだとののしってあざ笑います。このふたりの「ムフ、

Picture Book of the Taikō) in the Amagasaki scene, where Takechi Mitsuhide sees his mother, Satsuki, and his son Jūjirō slain before his very eyes, and weeps bitterly.

During these moments when the *tayū* is putting his heart and soul into the narration, the shamisen player is by no means idle. He plucks the shamisen strings with a particular vigor, in a manner referred to as *tataki-bachi* (hitting). He also lets his plectrum strike the skin stretched over the bowl of his instrument to produce an emotive thudding sound.

Q **The laughter performed by the *tayū* is remarkable. What are the ways in which this laughter is used?**

Warai (scenes of laughter) where the *tayū* laughs on and on till he runs out of breath, always leave a very strong impression on bunraku audiences.

There are several famous such laughter scenes. One occurs in *Sugawara Denjū Tenarai Kagami*, where Fujiwara no Shihei, who is Sugawara's rival and enemy, laughs. In this play, Sugawara no Michizane is stripped of his office through Shihei's scheming, after which the play continues to its tragic denouement.

Shihei's laughter occurs in the Stopping the Carriage scene, where he scornfully refers to Umeomaru and Sakuramaru, Sugawara's retainers, men who are unswerving in their loyalty to Sugawara, as "you little maggots."

Another *warai* scene occurs in *Kanadehon Chūshingura* (The Treasury of Loyal Retainers), when Kōno Moronao laughs. In the third act, Moronao heaps insults on En'ya Hangan, calling him a stupid carp, and laughing at him sneeringly. The

ハハ、ムフ、ハハ」と延々と続く笑いが、あ
ざ笑いとして有名です。

　悲しみと喜びが交差する笑いが「菅原伝授
手習鑑」の「寺子屋」の松王丸の笑いです。

　親の代から菅原道真に恩のある松王丸の子
が、道真の息子の秀才の身代わりに命を落と
しますが、その死の様子を聞かされた松王丸
は、悲しみを押し隠して笑います。

この悲痛な笑いが観客の胸を打ちます。

**三味線弾きは義太夫とどういう掛け合いで
伴奏しているのでしょうか?**

　A 義太夫節は必ず三味線の独奏から始まり
ます。文楽では、この冒頭の演奏を「弾出し」
といっており、義太夫と一緒の演奏を「枕」
といいます。「枕」では三味線が少しずつ先
を弾き、太夫がそれに付いて行くのが理想的
だと言われています。

左から太棹、中棹、細棹

　三味線は太棹といって、三味線の中でも一
番胴も糸も太い物を用います。長唄などに用
いられる細棹や、清元などに用いられる中棹
に比べて、腹にずんと染み入るような重く強
い音が出るのが特徴です。その三味線へのバ
チの当て方1つで、雪や夜などの情景から、
主人公の喜怒哀楽の気持ちまでを表現するわ
けです。

laughter of the two men, which continues on and on, is a celebrated example of derisive laughter in bunraku.

Another *warai* scene, where the laughter is criss-crossed with sorrow, occurs in *Sugawara Denju Tenarai Kagami*, in the Village School scene. In this scene, Matsuomaru is informed that his son, indebted to the nobleman Sugawara no Michizane on account of his father, has sacrificed his life to save Michizane's son Shūsai. In an effort to disguise the profound grief that grips him when he hears the news, Matsuomaru bursts out laughing. Matsuomaru's heart-rending, bitter laughter is always deeply affecting for the audience.

 Q **What kinds of accompaniment does the shamisen provide for the *gidayū*?**

Gidayū-bushi invariably commences with a solo passage from the shamisen player. In bunraku, this introductory passage is called the *hikidashi* (lead-in). The sections where the narration is accompanied by the shamisen are referred to as *makura*, or "pillow" sections. In *makura* sections, the ideal is held to involve a gradual progression, with the shamisen player playing a few notes, and the *gidayū* then commencing his narration.

The *futozao* shamisen used in bunraku is the largest shamisen available, both in its body and in the gut used for its strings. This instrument produces a much heavier and more resonant tone when plucked than the more delicate *hosozao* and *nakazao* shamisen, used in either *nagauta* or Kiyomoto chanting. Its sound is truly penetrating. A single stroke with the plectrum over the strings of this instrument is sufficient to evoke snow falling or an evening scene, or to signify any one of a variety of moods and emotions.

人形と人形遣い

Q 人形は何人で動かすのですか。

三人遣い
（左から、主遣い、
足遣い、左遣い）

A 近松門左衛門が活躍していた時代には、1人の人形遣いが1つの人形を動かしていました。ところが観客も次第に人形に対して複雑な動きを求め出します。その結果、3人で1体の人形を動かすようになってきました。

1人は人形の右手と首を動かします。中心となる人で、「主遣い」と言われています。ほかの2人は、1人が左手を動かし、「左遣い」と呼ばれます。もう1人が足を動かし、「足遣い」と呼ばれます。これによって、1人で人形を動かすよりもずっと細かい動きをさせることが可能となりました。

Q 文楽の人形はどんな作りになっているのですか。

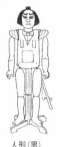

人形（男）

A 文楽の人形は首と胴、手、足から出来ています。複雑な動きをする人形ですから、構造も複雑に違いないと思われるでしょうが、実は人形の仕掛けはごく単純なものなのです。

首はヒノキ（檜）の木彫りで、一番大きなもので縦15センチ、横10センチほどです。女形は一回りほど小さくなっています。ツメという端役の1人で遣う人形以外は、首の中が

PUPPETS AND PUPPETEERS

 How many puppeteers manipulate each doll?

During the age in which Chikamatsu Monzaemon was active, each doll was manipulated by one puppeteer. But gradually, audiences came to want more and more complex movements from the dolls, which is why three puppeteers came to be used.

One puppeteer is responsible for the right arm and the head of the puppet. He is the most important of the three and is referred to as the *omo-zukai* (main puppeteer). Of the other two, one is responsible for moving the left arm: he is the *hidari-zukai* (left puppeteer). The other puppeteer is responsible for manipulating the puppet's feet: he is referred to as the *ashi-zukai* (foot puppeteer). With this division of labor, it became possible to make the dolls perform infinitely more intricate maneuvers than before.

 How are bunraku dolls constructed?

Bunraku dolls consist of a head, body, hands, and feet. People tend to assume that since the dolls make such intricate movements, they must have lots of complex gadgetry—but, in fact, the dolls are exceedingly simple in their construction.

The puppets' heads are carved out of *hinoki*, or Japanese cypress. The largest of the heads can be up to fifteen centimeters high and ten centimeters wide, though the heads of female puppets are markedly smaller. Apart from the *tsume* (heads

くりぬいてあり、その中でも、立役（芝居の男性の役）の場合は、目、眉、口などが動くようになっています。立役の首は役によって白、卵色（黄色）、赤などに彩色します。

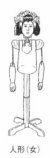

人形（女）

女形の人形はほとんどが白で、老女の役は薄い卵色に塗ります。顔は目の開閉ができるぐらいで、ほとんどの場合、立役のように複雑な仕掛けはありません。

首と胴は「胴串」という仕掛けのある棒でつながれます。人間で言えば背骨にあたるこの棒が、人形では重要な役割を果たします。

胴串には溝があり、口を開けたり、目を閉じたりといった首の仕掛けを操る糸が通っています。糸の先には栓が付いていて、首をうなずかせる時にこの栓を引きます。この栓のことを「チョイ」と言います。

仕掛けを動かす時のバネにはセミクジラの髭が使用されています。まだ買い置きがあるそうですが、捕鯨は制限されていますから、いずれなくなるのではないかと心配されています。

人形の首と右手を動かす主遣いは、自分の左手を人形の背中から入れて、この胴串を持ち、胴串の下に掌をあて、小指と薬指で胴串を握って人形を支えます。

that go on dolls for very minor parts), which are manipulated by one person, the dolls' heads will all have been chiseled out inside, making it possible to move the eyes, eyebrows, and mouth of those heads that go on *tate yaku* (major male roles). The heads for these male roles are painted with a variety of colors—white, yellow or red—depending on the characteristics of the part.

The heads for nearly all dolls in female roles are white, though those for old women are painted in a color that is slightly yellow. The female heads are almost all capable of opening and shutting their eyes, but very few of them can do anything more complicated than that.

The head is fitted onto the body by means of a pole, known as the *dogushi*, which has a certain amount of gadgetry. This pole occupies a place in the doll comparable to the backbone in a human being; and much like the backbone, it plays a vital role.

The fittings on the *dogushi* consist of a groove, along the length of which lie the strings to control the various devices that do things like open the doll's mouth, or close the eyes. The ends of the strings have *choi* (toggles) which are pulled to produce various actions.

These mechanisms rely on springs manufactured out of the whiskers of a particular kind of whale. Though some stock remains, the ban on whaling has led to fears of the supply of these running out sooner or later.

The *omo-zukai*, the puppeteer who operates the doll's head and right arm, supports the doll by standing by it and gripping the *dogushi* with his left hand, which he will have put inside the doll from behind. He wraps his palm around the lower end of the *dogushi*, gripping it between his third and little fingers.

　人形の胴は「肩板」という真ん中に胴串を通すための穴が開いた板と、人間で言えば腰にあたる「腰輪」という竹製の輪からできています。胴の前後には布が垂らしてあり、肩板の両端にはヘチマをつけてあり、これで肩の丸みを出します。胴の中は空っぽで、衣装を付けることで肉体を表現するわけです。胴の大きさは性別や役柄によって異なります。

　人形の手足は肩板からひもでぶら下げてあります。おもしろいのは、女形の人形には足がないことです。衣装の裾をうまく遣って、まるで足があるかのように見せるのです。

 人形の首にはどんな種類がありますか。

　A 首には、老人、男性、女性、子供など40種類ほどがあります。男性の役の立役が20数種類、女性の役の女形が約10種類です。これだけで、ほとんどの役柄の年齢、容姿、性格をカバーしています。

　狂言が決まり、どんな役が登場するかがはっきりすると、どの役にどの首を使用するかという「首割り」が行われます。首が決まればその役の性格付けが決まります。人形遣いはその性格にふさわしい遣い方を要求されるわけですから、首割りとはそれだけ重要なことなのです。

The doll's body consists of a wooden board, known as the *kata-ita* (shoulder blade board), which has a hole in the middle for the *dogushi* to go through, and a hoop of bamboo for what in a human being would be the hip region. Cotton strips hang in front and back, and sponge gourds are attached along both edges of the *kata-ita* so that the shoulders have some fullness. But the actual body of the doll is an empty space: the doll's costume provides the sense of physical flesh. The size of the body will vary according to the sex of the doll, as well as the requirements of the part.

The doll's feet dangle from strings attached to the shoulder-blade board. Interestingly, dolls in female roles don't actually have feet: the hems of their robes are simply moved in a way that gives the impression that they do.

 ## Q What are the varieties of heads for bunraku dolls?

There are about forty different types of heads for bunraku dolls—heads for old people, men, women, children, and many more. These include over twenty types of heads for male figures in major roles, and about ten types for dolls in female roles. With such a choice, the different possibilities for all roles in terms of age, looks and character are more or less covered.

Once it has been decided which play is to be performed, and thus which characters are to be involved, it then has to be determined which heads are to be used for the particular roles. This process is called *kashira-wari* (literally, the apportioning of heads). Since the head of a doll has an irrevocable effect on the character of the role, the apportioning of heads is a matter of no small consequence, with a decisive influence on the way

文七

立役の首の代表的なものとして、太い眉に大きな目、引き締まった口元の男性の頭があります。口は動きません。これは「文七」と呼ばれます。大坂の侠客・雁金文七の人形に用いたのが始めとされます。「菅原伝授手習鑑」の松王丸など、知識があり武勇に優れた主役級の人間に多く用いられます。

おなじ文七でも、口が開く首があります。こちらは「菅原伝授手習鑑」の藤原時平など天下を狙う大悪人に使用します。文楽の大悪人は人をあざけって大笑いする場合が多いため口が開くように作られているのです。

団七

源太

男性の顔として、目が大きくてあごが張っているものもあります。時代物の武将など、勇ましい役柄に遣います。これを「大団七」と言います。大団七を小さくしたのが「小団七」と言って、こちらは世話物の小悪党の役に遣います。例えば「義経千本桜」のいがみの権太などに用います。

優しく美しい顔をしているものを「源太」と言います。女性にもてる役柄で、「仮名手本忠臣蔵」の勘平などに遣います。

そのほか、理知的で分別のある役柄に遣うもの、穏やかで頭のいい人に遣うもの、年配の男性に遣うもの、敵役ではあるがちょっと愛嬌のある役に遣うもの、などなど多彩で、

娘

a puppeteer will have to manipulate his doll.

A typical head for a male figure in a major role is Bunshichi, named after the role for which it is said to have first been used, an Ōsaka gallant named Karigane Bunshichi. This head has bushy eyebrows, large eyes, and a very firm-set mouth. The mouth does not open. It is frequently used for dolls in male roles, for men of intelligence who are also very brave, such Matsuomaru in *Sugawara Denju Tenarai Kagami*.

Another Bunshichi head is exactly the same, except for the fact that its mouth does open. This head is used for evil, ambitious men, such as Fujiwara no Shihei in the above-mentioned play *Sugawara Denjū Tenarai Kagami*. Frequently, in bunraku, these mean-spirited villains will laugh at people, covering them with scorn, which makes it necessary for the mouth to be able to open.

Another head used for puppets in male roles has very large, glaring eyes, and a wide, full chin. This one is used for men of courage and valor, for example, generals in *jidaimono* (historical plays). This particular head is known as Dai Danshichi. Another, smaller version is called Shō Danshichi, and is used for rascally male roles in *sewamono* (plays about the affairs of ordinary people), for example, Igami no Gonta in *Yoshitsune Sembon Zakura*.

One head with a gentle, handsome expression is Genta. This head is used for young, good-looking men, and is often used for the young retainer Kanpei in *Kanadehon Chūshingura*.

There are numerous other heads for dolls in male roles, each with its own name and its own peculiar characteristics: a head for a shrewd, intellectual man; a head for a clever but mild-natured man; heads for old men; and a head for an evil

老女形

それぞれ名前がつけられています。

しかし、女性の首は男性に比べると種類が
あまりありません。役柄というよりは年齢で
分けてあって、未婚で年若い女性用の「娘」、
既婚で年配の女性用の「老女形」に大きく分
けられます。お姫様も町娘もすべて娘の首、
大名の奥方も商店の女房もすべて年配の首で
す。

婆

この2種類の首は、口の部分に小さな針が
ついています。泣く表現では、ここに手ぬぐ
いなどをひっかけ、口でくわえて悲しみをこ
らえている様子を見せます。

傾城

もっと高齢で世話物の善良な女性などに遣
われるのが「婆」です。同様に高齢でも、い
じわるで怖い敵役の女性に遣われる首を「八
汐」と言います。そのほか、ぐっと華やかで
高級な遊女に遣う「傾城」、滑稽な役どころ
に遣う頬がぷっくりと膨らんで目の細い愛嬌
のある「お福」などがあります。

江戸時代にはほとんどの女性が20歳前に結
婚し、そのまま家庭に入りました。娘か妻か
遊女か。生き方の選択肢の少なさがそのまま、
首にも反映されていると見ていいでしょう。

お福

but still somehow attractive villain.

Compared to the wide variety of heads for dolls in male roles, dolls in female roles have much less choice. The heads for female dolls are also divided by age, rather than personality, into the two basic categories of *musume* (young, unmarried women) and *fuke-oyama* (married, older women). Girls of high birth together with ordinary town girls are given the same unmarried *musume* head, and wives of *daimyō* or shopkeepers' wives are given the same head as that used for the older woman.

Both types of heads for female roles will have a small pin sticking out near the lips. This is for weeping scenes, to catch the cloth or handkerchief the doll will hold up to her mouth, making it appear as if she is biting down on it in a vain attempt to restrain her grief.

There is also *baba* (granny head), used for old women who are kind-hearted, and a head called Yashio, used for spiteful, vicious old women. There is *keisei*, a head used for splendidly attired, high-ranking courtesans, as well as *O-Fuku*, the head used for humorous female characters. This head has large, round cheeks and smiling eyes that exude warm affection.

During the Edo period (1600–1868) most women married at around twenty, and "entered the home." A woman was either unmarried or married ... or else a woman of the pleasure quarters. It is probably correct to regard the scarcity of choice for heads of female dolls as a true reflection of the scarcity of options for women in the possibilities for lifestyles.

人形の手は小さいのに、ずいぶん器用に動きますが、一体どういう仕掛けになっているのでしょう。

A 手にもいろいろな種類があり、これも立役と女形では違います。

まず、手首は動きますが指は動かないものがあります。これを「かせ手」といって、立役で代表的なものです。さらに5本の指が動くのがあり、これを「つかみ手」と言います。つかみ手で手首が動くのを「たこつかみ」、指が開くのを「かきつばた」と言うなど、それぞれに名称がつけられています。

女形には、「女手」あるいは「もみじ手」と呼ばれる1種類しかありません。親指と4本の指に分かれ、3段に折れる仕掛けです。立役の手に比べると、小さく繊細にできています。

 人形は役柄によってどんな衣装を着ますか。

A 人形の作りのところで説明したように、人形の胴は空っぽになっています。この空っぽの胴に衣装を着けて、肉体を表現するわけです。

文楽の衣装は絹製です。女形でもお姫様は赤系統の衣装、年配の女房役は小豆色系統の地味な色と決まっています。茶色は老人の役に使うのが一般的です。人形の衣装で一番特

Q The hands of the dolls are capable of such delicate movements, despite their small size. What makes them so dexterous?

There are also all sorts of varieties of hands. Here, too, there are differences in the hands for dolls in male and female roles.

Firstly, we might mention the type of hand where the wrist can be made to bend, but not the fingers. This type is called the *kase-te* (waving hand), and is typically used for dolls in male roles. But there are other types, too, each with its own name. Hands where the fingers can move but not the wrist are known as the *tsukami-te* (grasping hand). The type where both wrist and fingers can be made to move is called the *tako-tsuka-mi* (octopus-grasper), and the hand whose fingers can spread, the *kakitsubata* (iris).

Dolls in female roles have only one variety of hand, called *onna-de* (female hand) or *momiji-te* (maple-leaf hand). These hands are divided between the thumb and fingers, the fingers being further divided into three separate sections that can bend. These women's hands are smaller and more graceful than the hands for male dolls.

 Q What are the kinds of costumes worn by bunraku puppets?

As explained in the section on the doll's composition, the body is actually an empty space. It is the costume that fits over the empty frame that provides the sense of a body.

Bunraku costumes are all made of silk. Dolls in female roles will wear red if they are young ladies of noble birth; older women will wear more sober, maroon colors. Dolls in elderly roles generally wear brown. A common aspect of all the dolls'

徴的なことは、主遣いが手を差し入れるための穴が背中に開いていることです。

　衣装が決定すると、それを人形の胴に縫い付けます。胴は人形遣いがそれぞれ個人で所有しており、前側の布に名前が書いてあります。衣装は公演ごとに人形遣いが、遣う人形に縫い付けます。最初に衿を合わせ、着物がはだけないようにふとん針で丁寧に縫い付けていきます。胴に衣装を付けた後に、足と手を吊って頭を胴串に差すと、人形の出来上がりです。

Q 人形遣いはどうやって人形を動かすのですか。

　A 現代の文楽の人形は3人で遣います。リーダーとなる「主遣い」は人形の背中から左手を差し込んで、胴串を持ち、右手で人形の右腕を持ちます。人形が扇や刀などの小道具を持つ時には、右手にある指革に指を通して自分で持ちますが、人形が持っているかのように見せます。

　「左遣い」は人形の左手を、「差金」という棒を右手で持って動かします。差金は人形の左腕の真ん中についています。左手は人形の胴体を客席から見えないように支えています。

costumes is that they will always have an opening in the back, through which the *omo-zukai* (puppeteer) puts his arm to hold the doll.

Once the costumes have been decided upon, they have to be sewn onto the dolls' torsos. These doll torsos are all individually owned by the puppeteers, whose names will be written on the strips of cloth that hang in front. With every new performance, the puppeteers sew the costumes onto the particular torso they will use. First, the two sides of the costume's neck are neatly aligned. Then, they are carefully stitched into place with a mattress needle in a way that will keep them from falling open. Once the robe is attached to the doll's frame, the hands and feet are then hung from the shoulder-blade board, and the doll's head fitted over the *dogushi*. The puppet is thus complete.

Q What is involved in the manipulation of the dolls?

In present-day bunraku, three puppeteers manipulate each doll. The *omo-zukai*, who provides the lead, holds the doll's central pole, or *dogushi*, from behind in his left hand. With his right hand he holds the right hand of the doll. When the doll has to hold a prop, like a fan or a sword, the puppeteer will slip his fingers through a small loop on the doll's right hand and hold it himself, but the effect is so lifelike that it will truly seem as if the puppet itself is grasping the object.

The *hidari-zukai* (puppeteer on the left) moves the puppet's left arm with his right hand, with the aid of a small rod known as the *sashi-gane*. This *sashi-gane* is attached to the left hand of the puppet. With his left hand he will be supporting the torso of the puppet in a way that is undetectable by the audience.

「足遣い」は人形の足を遣います。立役の人形の場合は、足の後ろについた「あり金」を両手で持って動かします。女形は足がないため、衣装の裾を中指と人差し指ではさみ、動いているかのような裾さばきを見せます。

立て膝などをして膝の厚みがないとおかしい場合には、足遣いが右手でこぶしを作り着物の中に入れて膝に見せます。

人形遣いの修業は足遣いから始まり、次に左遣い、そして主遣いと進んでいきます。修業は厳しく、「足十年、左十年」と言われます。人形は立役の重いものですと10キロ以上あります。それを主遣いは左手だけで支えるわけです。主遣いは二の腕を水平にして肘を曲げて人形を持ちます。人形を前屈みにならずに真っ直ぐに保つためには、背を反らせた状態でいなければなりません。3人が息を1つに合わせないと文楽の人形は、命あるものとして動いてはくれないのです。主遣いの下にどの左遣い、足遣いが入るかは原則として公演ごとに決められます。

人形遣いは、基本的には3人とも黒衣を着用し、顔を見せませんが、重要な場面では主遣いだけが顔を出します。

The *ashi-zukai* (foot puppeteer) is responsible for movement of the doll's feet. For dolls in male roles, he will move each foot by holding a small rod, or *ari-gane*, attached to the heel. Dolls in female roles, however, do not possess feet, so here the puppeteer has to pinch the hem of the doll's skirt between forefinger and middle finger to produce a back-and-forth movement that suggests the presence of feet.

Sometimes the dolls will have to sit in various positions—with one knee drawn up, for example—which require that the knee area be given a certain bulk to look natural. The *ashi-zukai* will then make his right hand into a fist and put it into the doll's robe, to give the effect of a knee.

Training in doll manipulation begins with the feet, as an *ashi-zukai*. One works one's way up to become a *hidari-zukai*, and finally, an *omo-zukai*. The years of apprenticeship are long and hard. As the saying goes, "ten years on the feet, ten years on the left." The dolls can be heavy, those for male roles weighing more than ten kilos. The *omo-zukai* has to support this weight with his left arm only, keeping the arm bent at the elbow and completely horizontal. In order to keep the doll perpendicular to the floor and to prevent it from drooping forward, he himself has to maintain a continually leaning-back position. The timing and coordination among the three puppeteers must be perfect for the puppet to move in a way that seems natural. The members of each team of puppeteers are generally decided upon with every new performance.

The puppeteers all wear black robes and, as a rule, they cover their faces. In the most important scenes, however, the main puppeteer's face will be uncovered.

Q 人形はまるで人間のように動きまわりますが、どんなふうに動かしているのでしょうか。

A 文楽の人形は人形遣いが動かしているため、平面の上にいるように見えても、実は宙に浮いた状態にあります。それを地上を歩いているように見せるための工夫が生まれました。

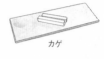

カゲ

1つは、人形がいい形でポーズを決める「見得」を切ったり、走ったりする際に、拍子木を板に打ち付けて音を出すことです。歌舞伎ではこれを「ツケ」と言いますが、文楽ではこれを「カゲ」と称します。歌舞伎は舞台が平面ですので、「ツケ」を打つ人も舞台の上に登場しますが、文楽の場合は平らな舞台ではないので、人に見えない場所、つまり陰に隠れているわけです。

もう1つは人形の足音である「足拍子」を使う方法です。しかし、人形は宙を浮いているのですから、足音が出る道理はありません。というわけで、人形の代わりに足音をさせるのは足遣いの仕事です。音は人形の側でしますから、観客からはちょうど人形が足音を立てているように聞こえます。

「足拍子」は、悲しみや憤りなど激しい感情表現の場合によく用います。女形の人形が不実な夫を恨み嘆く時、恋しい男の元へ飛んで行こうとする時、この足拍子が使われます。普段はおとなしい女性の感情の爆発を効果的に彩る技法と言えます。

Q **The dolls seem to move and walk just like human beings. What is involved in their presentation?**

Bunraku dolls may appear to be moving about on a flat surface, but of course, since they are moved and held by puppeteers, they are in fact suspended in midair. Certain measures have thus to be taken in order to strengthen the effect that the puppets are walking on the ground.

One of these methods involves a pair of wooden clappers being struck to produce a clatter whenever the dolls run (when they strike a climactic pose, known as *mie*). In kabuki, the clappers are called *tsuke*; in bunraku, *kage*. In kabuki, the stage is an actual flat surface, so the person who strikes the wooden clappers makes an appearance. In bunraku, however, since there is no such flat surface, the clappers are struck out of the spectators' view.

Another device is the sound that is made to reproduce the doll's footsteps, known as *ashi-byōshi*. Since in reality the doll is hanging off the ground, in midair, it is out of the question for it to make any sound. It is thus the job of the *ashi-zukai* to produce the sound instead of the doll. Though he produces it off to the doll's side, to the audience it seems just as if the sound is coming from the doll's feet.

Ashi-byōshi is also used when a doll expresses strong emotion, such as grief or indignation. When a female doll expresses resentment of her faithless husband, or when she attempts to dash over to the man she loves—at such times, the *ashi-byōshi* will be employed. It is an effective way of highlighting a sudden outburst of feeling in an otherwise placid, well-behaved woman.

「足拍子」や「カゲ」は、主遣いとはもちろん、太夫、三味線とも間合いが合わなければ失敗です。人形遣いにとって重要な修業の1つともなっているのです。

Q 女形の人形を見ていて本当に美しいと思いましたが、美しく見せるための工夫を教えて下さい。

A 人形が人間と違うのは言うまでもありません。その人形を人間以上に、美しく見せるために、人形遣いは人間には決してできない動きを人形にさせました。

1つは、頭（文楽では「ず」と読みます）を右、左に「動かす」ことで、「クリズ」と言います。これは女性の感情が高まった時に使います。右に動かす場合は、1度左に頭をやってから右へ回し、左に動かす場合は、1度右に頭をやってから左へ回します。こうすれば、単に左右に顔を動かすよりは、観客に一層印象づけられます。

もう1つが、後ろ向きになってポーズを決めることです。「ウシロブリ」と言います。この動きは、辛さ、切なさを表現するために、上記の「クリズ」と一緒に使われます。この動きをするのは女形だけで、女性美を象徴化したものとされています。

「ウシロブリ」の際に、主遣いは、人形の右手を左遣いにまかせて正面を向き、左手だけで人形を支えて人形の後ろ姿を観客に見せま

In *ashi-byōshi* and *kage*, the timing with the *omo-zukai* as well as with the *tayū* and shamisen has to be absolutely perfect for the appropriate effect. Such moments thus form important points for puppeteers in the mastery of their art.

 Q Some of the dolls in female roles possess an exquisite beauty. What are some of the techniques involved in their presentation?

It goes without saying that dolls and human beings are quite different. In order to make a doll in a female role appear even more alluring than a real woman, the puppeteer will have had to make the doll perform some actions that no humans ever perform in real life.

One of these involves moving the head (the *zu* in bunraku) to the right or left, referred to as *kuri-zu*. This is a movement that a doll will make in moments of extreme passion. To make the head move right, it is first brought left and then swung right, whilst to make the head move left, it is first brought right. Such preliminary measures work to accentuate the movement for the audience.

Another movement involves the puppet turning her back to the audience and adopting a pose. This is called *ushiro-buri* (a turn to the rear), and it is used in combination with the above *kuri-zu* to express grief or sorrow. These moves are reserved solely for dolls in female roles, and they are considered to express the epitome of female beauty.

In an *ushiro-buri*, the *omo-zukai* (main puppeteer) will give the right hand of the doll to the *hidari-zukai* (puppeteer on the left). Still facing stage front and supporting the doll with his

す。左遣いは人形の両方の袖を左右に一杯に
広げます。この形で静止した人形の美しさは
えも言われぬもので、観客がうっとりとする
場面です。

体をねじる動きも女性の人形特有です。人
形が相手に激しく詰め寄る場面などに用いま
す。前傾姿勢で乗り出すようにして体を相手
の方にねじります。これを「ネジ」と言いま
す。

Q 文楽の舞台の構造は、歌舞伎などの芝居の舞台とは
違うのでしょうか。

舞台下駄

A 文楽は1人遣いから3人遣いへとなりまし
た。足遣いが中腰で足を遣うためには、主遣
いの背が高くなる必要があります。そこで主
遣いは舞台下駄という高さが20センチから50
センチもあるような下駄を履きます。

しかし、観客が高いところで動く人形を仰
ぎ見る格好になるとおかしいので、文楽では
舞台の前方を約36センチ掘り下げてありま
す。「船底」と呼びますが、ここで人形遣い
は人形を動かします。

そして舞台の最前方、船底の前、船底の後
ろにそれぞれ板を立てます。足遣い、主遣い、
左遣いの足元を隠し、人形が平らな所で動い
ているように見せるための工夫です。この板
を「手摺」と呼びます。

left arm, he will allow the audience a view of the puppet's back. Meanwhile, the *hidari-zukai* will spread the arms of the dolls wide and display her kimono sleeves. The beauty of the doll as she holds this position is indescribable, and such scenes always send the spectators into raptures.

Another action peculiar to female dolls is a squirming movement, used when the doll is sidling in on another person with particular intensity. At a slightly pitched angle, the doll will thrust herself, squirming, over to the other person, almost as if to leap on them. The action is called *neji* (twisting).

 Q What are the features of the bunraku stage?

Although originally in bunraku each puppet was manipulated by one puppeteer, eventually three people came to be used. Since the *ashi-zukai* manipulates the puppet's feet in a half-standing, crouched position, the *omo-zukai* (lead puppeteer) has to be able to stand on a higher level. Accordingly, the *omo-zukai* wears extra tall *geta*, or clogs, which can be anything from twenty to fifty centimeters high.

Even so, it would be strange for the spectators to have to sit looking up at the dolls, so the front portion of the bunraku stage is laid with a pit about thirty-six centimeters deep. This is referred to as the *funazoko* (ship's bottom) and is where the puppeteers stand as they manipulate the dolls.

Further, at the front of the stage, just in front of the *funazoko*, and also just behind it, are palisades. These are designed to conceal the lower half of the puppeteers as they manipulate the dolls, so that the dolls can appear to be walking on a flat surface. They are called *tesuri* (railings).

　人形を遣う時に、大切なのは、前から2枚目の手摺りで、客席からはここが地面で、人形はこの「二の手」の上を歩いているように見えなければなりません。

　歌舞伎の大道具にあたる建物などの屋体は、上から吊ってあります。

　舞台の上手(右側)と下手(左側)には幕がかかっています。「小幕」といい、歌舞伎で言えば揚幕で、ここから人形は出入りします。開閉は人形遣いがします。太夫と三味線弾きの座る床は上手に設けられ、幕は歌舞伎とは逆に下手から上手へ向かって引かれます。

演者たちと文楽の興行

 文楽で有名な太夫、三味線弾き、人形遣いにはどんな人がいましたか。

　A 文楽では一座を代表する太夫のことを「櫓下」あるいは「紋下」と呼びました。

　文楽では興行のつど「番付」といって、演目や出演者の名前を書いた刷り物を配りました。番付では太夫、三味線、人形遣いの名が序列にもとづいて書かれます。この番付で一座を代表する太夫は一番右側の座紋の下に書かれました。また劇場の「櫓」の下にも一枚看板で掲げました。それで「櫓下」「紋下」と言われるようになったわけです。

As they manipulate the dolls, the puppeteers have to make it seem to the audience that the area just behind the second palisade, known as the *ni no te*, is the ground on which the dolls are walking and moving.

Scaffolding for buildings, which in kabuki would belong in the category of large theatrical props, hang from the stage flies.

On stage, small curtains hang to the left and right. These are known as *komaku* (*agemaku* in kabuki). It is through these that the dolls make their entrances and exits. The puppeteers are responsible for moving the curtains aside. To the right of the stage is a dais for the narrator and shamisen player. The stage curtain in bunraku is drawn open from left to right, unlike kabuki, where the opposite is the case.

BUNRAKU PLAYERS AND BUNRAKU PERFORMANCE

Q Who were some celebrated narrators, shamisen players, and puppeteers in bunraku?

In the old days in bunraku, the top *tayū* in a theater would be given the designation of *mon-shita* (below the crest) narrator, or *yagura-shita* (below the turret) narrator.

The names derive from a time when *banzuke* (playbills) would be handed out, listing the titles of plays and the names of the performers and players in order of rank. The top narrator's name would appear immediately after the theater's crest, on the right-hand side of the playbill. It would also appear on the announcements hanging from the turret of the theater.

文楽でほかをリードするのが太夫です。だから、紋下は通常の場合、太夫から選ばれました。しかし、文楽が「文楽協会」の運営となってから、この紋下制度はなくなりました。

最後の紋下となった太夫が、豊竹山城少掾です。明治11（1878）年に生まれ、昭和42（1967）年に亡くなりました。名人として知られ、現代の太夫のほとんどはその影響を受けています。

豊竹山城少掾

文楽の太夫は昭和28（1953）年からは「大夫」と表記しています。もとはすべて太夫でしたが、これを大夫と変えるべきだと主張したのが山城少掾です。太夫の語源は官職の「大夫」にあるのだから、「太夫」ではおかしいというのがその理由だったようです。ほかには竹本摂津大掾（1836–1917）、竹本綱太夫（1904–69）などが有名です。

三味線で名人として知られるのは豊沢団平（1828–98）です。三味線弾きとして優れていたのはもちろん、作曲の才能にも恵まれ、妻の千賀と「壺坂霊験記」などの人気作品を残しています。ほかには初代鶴沢道八（1869–1944）、二代目野沢喜左衛門（1891–1976）などが有名です。

人形遣いでは吉田玉造（1829–1905）が知られています。原則として太夫がなるはずの紋下に人形遣いとして初めてなった人です。ほかには吉田栄三（1872–1945）、吉田文五郎（1869–1962）などが有名です。

The *tayū*'s name was listed in the topmost position because he is the person who leads the play. Ever since bunraku came to be run under the auspices of the Bunraku Foundation, however, this particular system of ranking has fallen into disuse.

The last *tayū* to be designated a "below the crest" narrator was Toyotake Yamashiro no Shōjō (1878–1967). He was a consummate master of his art, and his influence can still be seen in the majority of narrators active nowadays.

In 1953, the way in which the word *tayū* was written was changed from 太夫 to 大夫. Originally, the word had been written as 太夫, but Yamashiro no Shōjō argued for the change, apparently giving as his reason the fact that the word *tayū* originally derived from *daifu*, the name of a government office in earlier centuries. Other celebrated narrators include Takemoto Settu no Daijō (1836–1917) and Takemoto Tsunadayū (1904–1969).

Toyozawa Danpei (1828–1898) is probably the most famous master shamisen player. Not only did he play the shamisen, he also composed for it. Among the many works he has left us is the well-known masterpiece *Tsubosaka Reigenki*, jointly composed with his wife Chika. Other celebrated shamisen players include Tsuruzawa Dōhachi I (1869–1944) and Nozawa Kizaemon II (1891–1976).

As far as puppeteers are concerned, Yoshida Tamazō (1829–1905) is the most famous. He was the first puppet manipulator ever to be listed as "below the crest," a designation previously reserved for the *tayū*, or narrator. Other celebrated puppeteers included Yoshida Eizō (1872–1945) and Yoshida Bungorō (1869–1962).

歌舞伎や能・狂言は、先祖代々同じ職業に
つく場合が多いようですが、文楽の太夫、三味線、
人形遣いもそうなのでしょうか。

A 古典芸能のうちで、文楽は最も世襲性の色が薄いものの1つでしょう。親が三味線弾きで、子が太夫といった例や、親も子も人形遣いという場合もありますが、ほとんどは外から入ってきた人たちです。師匠のもとに入門し、厳しい修業に耐えて芸を身に付けます。襲名でも、歌舞伎はほとんどの場合、子供や親類が継承します。ところが、文楽は、たとえ実子が同じ職業についていても、弟子の中から優れた者を選んで名前を継がせます。

文楽は、昭和47(1972)年から、国立劇場で後継者養成のための研修制度を始めました。研修生は一般公募で、2年間研修をうけた後に、太夫、三味線、人形遣いに分かれて、それぞれの師匠へ入門します。文楽にたずさわる人を「技芸員」と言いますが、研修所を経由せずに、直接、師匠に入門する人もいます。しかし現在ではそれは少数で、技芸員の約半分が研修生出身です。

Q In kabuki, nō and kyōgen, professions to do with the stage often seem to be passed on for generations within the same family. Is this true of bunraku, too?

Of all Japanese traditional performing arts, bunraku is probably the one in which hereditary succession is least in evidence. Occasionally, a father will be a shamisen player and his son a narrator, or both father and son will be puppeteers. But for the most part, performers come to bunraku from the outside. They enter into training under a master, and undergo an exacting apprenticeship, immersing themselves in their art. Hereditary succession to stage names is likewise unusual. Unlike in kabuki, where a famous actor's child or relative will often inherit his stage name, in bunraku, if selected, a particularly gifted student can succeed to the name of a famous performer regardless of whether the performer's own son is a member of the profession.

Since 1972, the Kokuritsu Gekijō (National Theater) has offered a system of in-house training for bunraku performers to foster successors, opening the doors to anyone interested in mastering the art. After two years in general theatrical duties, the trainees then divide up into narrators, shamisen players, or puppeteers, to enter into more specialized training under masters. These days, there are fewer *gigei-in* (the designation for any performer-artist involved in bunraku) who enter directly into apprenticeship under a master. About half the bunraku performers are products of the in-house trainee system.

日本舞踊、落語、講談、浪曲

Nihon Buyō, Rakugo, Kōdan, Rōkyoku

日本舞踊

Q 「日本舞踊」というのは、具体的には
どんな踊りを言うのでしょうか。

A 実は、「日本舞踊」という言葉を使い出
したのは明治時代の作家で学者の坪内逍遥で
す。それまでは「舞」、あるいは「踊り」と
言われていたものを1つにまとめて言ったわ
けです。一般に「舞」は旋回する動きを基本
に置き、「踊り」は跳ね上がる動きを基本に
していると言われます。

京鹿子娘道成寺

　舞や踊りは、古くは、宗教的儀式として行
われていたのでしょうが、歌舞伎の項でも説
明されているように、見世物としての舞踊が、
出雲の阿国によって生み出され、それがやが
て歌舞伎舞踊として発展していきます。

　歌舞伎の舞踊の振り付けは、当初は歌舞伎俳
優自身が行っていましたが、やがて専門の振付
家が登場するようになりました。その振付家の元
祖と言われるのが、元禄時代に活躍した初代中
村伝次郎です。伝次郎は志賀山流という流派を
起こし、これは現在まで続いています。

　続いて登場したのが初代西川扇蔵が始めた
西川流です。初代藤間勘兵衛が始めた藤間流
も江戸時代に生まれました。現在では藤間流
には勘十郎家と勘右衛門家の2つがあります。

　ほかによく知られた流派としては、幕末に

NIHON BUYŌ (JAPANESE CLASSICAL DANCE)

 What kind of dance is *nihon buyō*?

The expression *nihon buyō* (Japanese classical dance) was first used in the Meiji period (1868–1912) by the writer and scholar Tsubouchi Shoyo (1859–1935). *Buyō* is a compound word consisting of two characters expressing different kinds of dance: *mai* and *odori*. While *mai* is essentially a circling movement, the basic movement in *odori* is leaping or skipping.

Both *mai* and *odori* were performed at religious ceremonies from ancient times yet, as explained in the chapter on kabuki theater, *buyō* was only first presented as a performance in its own right in 1603, by Izumo no Okuni. These performances eventually developed into kabuki.

In kabuki, the choreography for *buyō* was originally done by the actors themselves, but in due course, specialist choreographers emerged. Nakamura Denjirō I, who was active in the Genroku era (1688–1704), is considered to be the originator of *buyō* choreography. He founded the Shigayama school, a tradition which has continued to this day.

The next important tradition to emerge was the Nishikawa school founded by Nishikawa Senzō I. The Fujima school, established by Fujima Kanbē I, is another tradition that had its beginnings in the Edo period (1600–1868). At present, the Fujima school has two families, the Kanjūrō family and the Kan'emon family.

Other well-known schools of *buyō* are the Hanayagi school,

初代花柳寿輔が始めた花柳流、坂東流、花柳流から別れた若柳流などがあります。主だった流儀のほとんどは、江戸の歌舞伎俳優や歌舞伎の振付家の創始になります。

Q 「座敷舞」とはどんなものですか。

A 西川流、藤間流、花柳流などが江戸に生まれた踊りなら、一方、上方(関西)で発達したのが、「座敷舞」と呼ばれる「舞」です。「踊り」が広い場所でたくさんの観客を相手に披露されるのに対し、座敷舞は、文字通りに料亭などの狭い座敷で、金屏風を後ろにして少数の観客に見せるものでした。

座敷舞

座敷舞は地唄で踊る「地唄物」と上方唄で踊る「端唄物」に大別されます。地唄は江戸時代の上方で、目の不自由な演奏家によって三味線などで演奏されました。能の作品を題材にしたものや、男女の恋に題材を取った作品などがあります。

前者では「葵の上」「鉄輪」「珠取海士」など、後者では「雪」などが有名です。

端唄は江戸時代の上方の流行歌です。地名を読み込んだり、歌舞伎狂言を題材にしたりした作品が多いようです。「綱は上意」「紀伊の国」などが知られています。

which was begun by Hanayagi Jusuke I at the end of the Tokugawa era in the mid-nineteenth century, the Bandō school, and the Wakayagi school, which broke away from the Hanayagi school. Most of the main schools of *buyō* were thus founded by kabuki actors or choreographers in the Edo period.

Q What is *zashiki-mai*?

While the Nishikawa, Fujima, and Hanayagi schools originated in Edo in east Japan, a different style of dance known as *zashiki-mai* (parlor dance) developed in the Kyōto-Ōsaka region in west Japan. While the *odori* style of dance was usually performed before a large audience in a wide space, this parlor dance, as the name implies, was performed in front of folding screens to just a few people, in small rooms at inns and the like.

Zashiki-mai can be broadly divided into two types: *jiuta-mono*, danced to local songs, and *hauta-mono*, danced to songs of the Kyōto-Ōsaka region. During the Edo period, *jiuta-mono* were performed in west Japan by blind singers, to the accompaniment of the shamisen. The dance themes were taken from nō plays or from love stories.

Examples of *jiuta-mono* are *Aoi no Ue* (Lady Aoi), *Kannawa* (Iron Wheels) and *Tamatoriama* (The Woman Pearl Diver), while *Yuki* (Snow) is an example of the *hauta-mono* style.

Hauta were popular songs in the Kyōto-Ōsaka region in the Edo period. Many of them included local place names and took their themes from kabuki or kyōgen. Well-known *hauta* are *Tsuna ha Jōi* (The Rope is Our Law) and *Kii no Kuni* (Kii Country).

落語

Q 「落語」とはどんなものですか。

A 落語家(あるいは噺家とも言います)と呼ばれる語り手が、1人で舞台の上の座布団に座って、ストーリー性のある面白い話をする話芸です。舞台に出てくるときは、三味線や太鼓による伴奏音楽(出囃子)に乗って登場します。

落語家は話の中で、声と身ぶり1つで、男にも女にも、年寄りにも子供にも、武士にも町人にもなります。首の向きを左右に変えるだけで違う人物に切り替わるのです。そして、手ぬぐいと扇子だけを小道具に、いろいろな状況を表現します。扇子は、杯にも、箸にも、刀にもなります。

江戸落語と呼ばれる東京の落語と上方落語と言われる関西の落語では、演じ方に若干の相違があります。

江戸落語

江戸落語は、芝居噺など特別な場合を除いては、音楽が入りませんが、上方落語は情景描写の時などに三味線や太鼓などのお囃子が入ります。お囃子には、おおむね、歌舞伎で、舞台の陰で演奏される音楽と同じ曲が使われます。

上方落語

また上方では、演者の前に見台と言われる小さな台が置いてあり、その前に膝をかくす

RAKUGO

 What is *rakugo*?

Rakugo is a comic monologue in which a storyteller (known as *rakugoka* or *hanashika*) sits atop a cushion on a stage and relates an episodic story. The entrance of the storyteller is announced by the *debayashi*, a brief flourish of shamisen and drum.

While telling his story, the *rakugo* performer can portray a man or woman, elderly person or child, samurai or townsperson by means of his voice or a single gesture, changing his role simply by turning his head to the left or right. His only props are a hand cloth and fan, which he skillfully employs to express various situations. The fan can be used to evoke different objects, such as a glass, chopsticks, or a sword.

There are slight but noticeable differences between the style of *rakugo* performed in Tōkyō, known as Edo *rakugo*, and the type performed in the Kyōto-Ōsaka region, known as Kamigata *rakugo*.

In Edo *rakugo*, apart from special cases such as stories based on plays, no music is played during the performance, whereas in Kamigata *rakugo*, musical accompaniment, known as *ohayashi* may be added to evoke certain emotions. This is usually the same as the music performed at the side of the stage during a kabuki play.

In Kamigata *rakugo*, the storyteller sits before a small stand known as the *kendai*, in front of which is a *tsuitate* (screen)

衝立を置きます。見台の左側には小さな拍子木がのせられ、右手には、外側を紙で包むように張った扇(これを「叩き」と言います)を持ち、要所要所でこの拍子木をたたいたり、扇で机をたたいたりして調子をとりながら、にぎやかに話を進めます。

Q 落語はいつごろ始まったのでしょうか。

A 落語の元祖は、江戸の初期におもしろい話を巧みな話術で語り聞かせた安楽庵策伝と言われています。策伝は天文23(1554)年に生まれた僧侶で、布教のために話芸を磨き、西日本を中心に、広く大衆に語りかけました。「醒睡笑」(「眠りを醒ます笑い」という意味)という笑い話を集めた本を残しています。策伝は、「落ち」または「さげ」という笑わせ所のある落語の基本的な形を確立させました。

策伝が寛永19(1642)年に亡くなった後に登場したのが、京都の露の五郎兵衛と、大坂の米沢彦八です。また江戸には鹿野武左衛門が有名でしたが、彼は幕府によって罪に問われ、元禄7(1694)年に大島へ島流しにされ、江戸の落語はしばらく中絶します。

江戸落語を復興したのは烏亭焉馬でした。焉馬は新作を披露する会を主宰し、落語の普及につとめました。その会から初代三遊亭円生、初代三笑亭可楽などが売り出し、再び江戸落語は盛んとなります。可楽は、観客から

that hides his knees. On the left-hand side of the *kendai* is a pair of wooden clappers and, in his right hand, the storyteller holds a fan covered on one side with *tataki* (paper). To keep the performance lively, he marks the rhythm of the words in the important parts of the story by beating the clappers or striking the *kendai* with his fan.

When did *rakugo* begin?

The originator of *rakugo* is said to be Anrakuan Sakuden, who gained renown in the early Edo period for his skillful storytelling. A Buddhist priest born in Tenmon 23 (1554), Sakuden honed his storytelling skills through his preaching and missionary work over a wide area, mainly in west Japan. His teachings were collected in a book of humorous anecdotes entitled *Seisuishō* (Laughs to Wake You Up). Sakuden established the basic *rakugo* form of the punch line, known as the *ochi* or *sage* (literally, "the drop").

After Sakuden's death in Kan'ei 19 (1642), the next important figures to appear were Tsuyu no Gorobē (1643–1703), in Kyōto, and Yonezawa Hikohachi (d. 1714), in Ōsaka. In Edo, one of the most famous *rakugo* performers was Shikano Buzaemon (1649–1699), but after he was prosecuted by the Tokugawa shogunate and exiled to the island of Ōshima in Genroku 7 (1694), Edo *rakugo* fell into abeyance.

The Edo *rakugo* tradition was revived by Utei Enba. Enba established a society for performing new works and worked hard to popularize *rakugo*. The society produced famous *rakugoka* such as Sanyūtei Enshō I and Sanshōtei Karaku I, and Edo *rakugo* flourished once again. Karaku was famous for

3つの題材を言ってもらって、その場で落語を作る「三題噺」を始めたことで有名です。

　落語は盛り場や神社や寺の境内に小屋を作ったり、料亭の座敷などで客を集めて語られていましたが、寛政時代（1789–1801）には、専用の劇場で、木戸銭という入場料を取って見せる「寄席」が誕生しました。大坂でも同じころに寄席が生まれたようです。

 落語にはどんな種類がありますか。

　A 終わりにしゃれや語呂合わせなどで面白く終わる「落とし噺」、庶民の人情を描いた「人情噺」、幽霊が出る「怪談噺」、芝居を題材にし、役者の声色などをまじえて演じる「芝居噺」などの古典落語と、大正時代以降に創作された新作落語があります。

　怪談噺は三笑亭可楽門下の初代林家正蔵が始めたと言われます。怪談噺では落語家が幽霊の面を被ったり、鳴り物を入れるなどの演出が行われます。芝居噺は初代円生が完成したとされます。高座の後ろに歌舞伎の舞台さながらの背景を置き、引き抜きの衣装や鳴り物などを使ったようです。

　人情噺は一般の落語よりも長く、落ちがないのが特色です。親子や夫婦の情愛などを描いた作品が多く、涙を誘う場面が設けられて

beginning the tradition of asking the audience for three themes and then composing *rakugo* on the spot. This was known as *sandai-banashi* (three-theme stories).

In the beginning, *rakugo* was performed in entertainment areas, temporary theaters in the precincts of shrines or temples, and in rooms in inns. The Kansei era (1789–1801) saw the establishment of *yose*, small *rakugo* theaters that charged an admission fee, called *kidosen*. *Yose* also appeared in Ōsaka at around the same time.

 What types of *rakugo* are there?

There are various types of *rakugo*. They can be broadly classified into two categories: classical *rakugo*, a broad category that includes *otoshi-banashi* (stories ending with a joke or pun), *ninjō-banashi* (stories portraying the human feelings of the common people), *kaidan-banashi* (ghost stories), and *shibai-banashi* (theatrical stories in which the storyteller mimics the actors' voices and faces); and new *rakugo*, produced from the Taishō period (1912–1926) onwards.

The tradition of telling ghost stories was begun by Hayashiya Shōzō, who was a pupil of Sanshōtei Karaku I. The storyteller wears a ghost mask, and the story is accompanied by music to create the appropriate mood. The performance of theatrical stories was perfected by Enshō I. A kabuki-like backdrop was set up at the back of the stage and different costumes and musical accompaniments were employed.

The tales of human compassion were generally longer and characterized by their lack of a comic punch line. Most of them were affecting stories portraying love between parents and chil-

います。日本の文芸作品が「笑い」よりも「涙」を重視して来たこと、歌舞伎の「世話物」の影響などが背景として考えられます。

　最も一般的な落語が落とし噺です。登場するのは町人や浪人などの庶民がほとんどです。大名が出てくる作品にしても、世間知らずで間が抜けている愛すべき主人公として描かれているのが主流です。

 落語はどんな構成になっているのでしょうか。

　A 通常は「枕(マクラ)」という導入部から始まり、本題に入って、最後は「落ち」になります。

　マクラでは、世間話や本題と接点のあるおもしろい話などをして、観客の気持ちを引きつけます。落語家がそれぞれ工夫をして観客を喜ばせますが、昔から工夫されたマクラ用の小咄をする場合もあります。

　落ちにはよく考えないとそのこっけいさが分からない落ちや、落語家のしぐさが落ちになっているもの、発音が似通っていても意味が違う駄じゃれが落ちになっているものなど、さまざまな種類があります。

dren or husbands and wives that would bring tears to the eyes of the audience. The tendency to emphasize the sad rather than the funny is thought to have largely come from the influence of Japanese literary works and *sewamono*, plays portraying the troubled lives of the common people, in the kabuki tradition.

The most common form of *rakugo* at the height of its popularity was the story with a comic ending. The characters portrayed in these stories were mostly ordinary people such as townspeople or *rōnin* (masterless warriors). Even in stories featuring a *daimyō* (feudal lord), the main protagonist was usually a lovable and funny character who knew little of the ways of the world.

Q How is a *rakugo* performance structured?

A *rakugo* performance generally begins with the storyteller's preliminary remarks, known as the *makura*. These are followed by the main story, which ends with the punch line.

The preliminary remarks serve to get the audience in the right mood with a piece of gossip or an amusing story in some way related to the main story. The storyteller uses various devices to please his audience, sometimes employing the traditional method of starting with a brief anecdote.

There are various kinds of punch lines, such as a subtle joke requiring some thought to appreciate it, a gesture instead of words, or a pun.

Q 落語には作者はいたのでしょうか。

三遊亭円朝

A ほとんどの落語は落語家たちが自分たちで創作してきた作品です。その中で出来の良い物が古典として継承されました。創作に優れた落語家として知られるのが、三遊亭円朝です。

円朝は、天保10(1839)年に江戸に生まれ、二代目三遊亭円生の弟子になりました。20歳ごろには、道具や鳴り物で背景に使う芝居噺で人気を集めましたが、当時、彼の属する三遊派は柳派に押されて振るわず、円朝はなんとか人気を盛り返そうと考えました。そこで、円朝は、派手な芝居噺を止め、扇と手ぬぐいだけで聞かせる落語に専念することになり、それが人気を得ました。

円朝は既に20代のころに「真景累ヶ淵」「怪談牡丹灯籠」などの怪談の傑作を書いていますが、新聞に掲載されたニュースなどを題材に落語の創作や人情噺の創作も始め、たくさんの人気作品を残しています。「怪談牡丹灯籠」や「真景累ヶ淵」「怪談乳房榎」などは歌舞伎にも取り入れられ、現在でもしばしば上演されています。

Q 落語家にはどんな序列がありますか。

A 落語家の修業は、師匠に入門するところから始まります。修業の最初が「前座」です。寄席での座布団の出し入れ、楽屋での師匠の

Are there specialist *rakugo* writers?

Most *rakugo* is written by the storytellers themselves. Among these, however, there are some classic *rakugo* that have been handed down through the generations. Sanyūtei Enchō is particularly well known for his outstanding *rakugo* compositions.

Born in Edo in Tempō 10 (1839), Enchō was apprenticed to Sanyūtei Enshō II. When he was about twenty, he was already popular for his *shibai-banashi* (theatrical stories), which used props and musical accompaniment. However, the Sanyū school to which he belonged declined in popularity with the rise of the Yanagi school, and Enchō had to find some way of reviving its fortunes. By abandoning melodramatic theatrical stories and concentrating on *rakugo* using simply a fan and hand cloth, he succeeded in restoring the popularity of the Sanyū school.

While still in his twenties, Enchō composed masterpieces of the ghost story genre such as *Shinkei Kasanegafuchi* and *Kaidan Botandōrō* (Ghost Story of the Peony Lantern). He also began the traditions of composing *rakugo* based on themes taken from newspapers and stories depicting human nature, leaving a rich legacy of popular *rakugo*. Works such as *Kaidan Botandōrō*, *Shinkei Kasanegafuchi*, and *Kaidan Chibusa-enoki* were adapted to kabuki and are still often performed today.

 What kind of ranking system is used in *rakugo*?

The training of a *rakugo* performer begins with his apprenticeship to a *rakugo* master, under whom he is appointed as a *zenza* (opening performer). At first, his main duties are to put

世話、ほかの落語家へのお茶の世話、出囃子の太鼓たたきなどから始まり、やがて正式な高座の前に一席語らせてもらえるようになります。

次が「二つ目」です。二つ目になると雑用からは解放され、寄席に出ても噺だけすればいいようになります。紋付きの着物の着用も許されます。

そして最後が落語家として一人前とみなされる「真打ち」です。昇進は能力と年限に応じて行われます。昇進した時に、それぞれの派に伝わる大きな名前に改名する場合もあります。

1日の高座で最後に話す真打ちの落語家を「トリ」といいます。また、大きな字で看板に書かれる格の高い落語家を「大看板」と呼びます。

 Q 落語はどこへ行けば聞けるのでしょうか。

A 東京の新宿にある末広亭、浅草にある浅草演芸ホール、千代田区隼町にある国立劇場演芸場、池袋にある池袋演芸場、上野にある上野鈴本演芸場などの寄席などで行われているほかに、あちらこちらのホールなどで、落語家が独演会を開いたりしています。

落語家の多くは組織に入っていて、大きな組織には、古典落語を得意とする落語家たちが中心の落語協会と、新作の落語をレパート

out the cushion on the stage at the *yose*, look after his master in the dressing room, prepare tea for other *rakugo* performers, beat the drum for *debayashi*, and so on. Eventually he is given the opportunity to tell a story in front of an audience before the start of the official performance.

The next rank is *futatsume* (number two). When the apprentice reaches this rank, he is released from his miscellaneous duties and is not required to do anything other than perform at the *yose*. He is also permitted to wear a crest on his kimono.

Finally, the *futatsume* is promoted to *shin'uchi*, a full-fledged principal performer, in accordance with his age and abilities. When he is promoted, he often changes his name to one of the traditional major names associated with the school to which he belongs.

A top storyteller who appears last at the end of a day's performance is known as a *tori*, and high-ranking performers whose names are written on posters in large characters are called *ōkanban*.

Q Where can you see *rakugo* today?

In addition to the shows at the five *yose* in Tōkyō—Suehiro-tei in Shinjuku, Asakusa Engei Hall in Asakusa, National Engeijō Theater in Hayabusachō in Chiyoda ward, Ikebukuro Engeijō in Ikebukuro, and Ueno Suzumoto Engeijō in Ueno—one-man *rakugo* performances are given at various halls and theaters.

Most *rakugo* performers belong to a certain organization. Among the larger organizations are the Rakugo Association, whose members are mainly performers specializing in classical

リーとする落語家が多い落語芸術協会があります。大阪には、上方落語教会があります。

講談

「講談」とはどんなものですか。

講談

A 落語と同様に「講釈師」と呼ばれる演者が、1人で台の前に座って、張り扇子という扇子で台をたたいて調子を取りながら、物語を語るのが講談です。江戸時代は講釈と呼ばれ、講談と言われるようになったのは明治に入ってからです。

落語のようにこっけいな話ではなく、戦争を材料として事実や空想をまじえた話や、敵討ちなどを話すのが特徴です。落語が会話を主体として構成されているのに対し、講談は、説明的な読み上げ口調で語られることを特徴とします。

室町時代にはすでに、諸国を回り、室町時代の軍記である「太平記」を読み聞かせる「太平記読み」が出現していました。その多くは戦国の世に主人を失った浪人者でした。また浪人の中には、新たな仕官先を求めて軍事についての講釈をして歩く者もいました。彼等の一部は江戸時代になると街頭で語り聞かせる芸人となり、やがて、講釈師が誕生し

rakugo, and the Rakugo Arts Association, consisting mostly of storytellers who perform new *rakugo* dating from the Taishō period (1912–1926). The main organization in Ōsaka is the Kamigata Rakugo Association.

KŌDAN

 What is *kōdan*?

Similar in many ways to *rakugo*, *kōdan* is performed by a *kōshakushi* (professional storyteller) who sits alone on stage in front of a desk and delivers a monologue while beating out the rhythm on the desk with a *harisensu* (fan). In the Edo period, this art was known as *kōshaku*; it came to be called *kōdan* during the Meiji period.

Unlike the comical stories of *rakugo*, *kōdan* is characterized by historical tales about war or revenge that combine fact and fiction. While *rakugo* is presented mainly in the form of a conversation, *kōdan* is distinguished by its expository style of recitation.

The Muromachi period (1333–1568) saw the appearance of storytellers who recited war tales from the *Taiheiki* (Chronicle of the Great Peace). These storytellers, known as *taiheiki-yomi*, were mostly *rōnin* (warriors) who had lost their masters during the Sengoku period of civil wars (1467–1568). By reciting historical tales in this way, some of these masterless warriors hoped to find new employers. By the beginning of the Edo period, certain of these storytellers had established themselves

ました。

　講釈師は知識人として尊敬され、将軍の前で軍記を講演する者もいました。江戸時代にはほかの話芸よりも一段高く見られました。講談以外の落語、漫才、曲芸などは、色どりとして上演される軽いものとみなされていたほどです。

Q どんな講釈師が活躍しましたか。

　A 固定化しつつある江戸時代の風潮に抗して、政治批判などの風刺に富んだ講釈を始め、大衆に歓迎されたのが深井志道軒です。

　同じころに活躍した講釈師に馬場文耕がいます。文耕は講談に、軍記物のほかに、町人社会の出来事や人物に取材した話や、お家騒動ものなどを取り入れたりして人気を博しましたが、幕府の政治を批判したというとがめを受けて処刑されました。しかし、志道軒と文耕の活躍により、講談は庶民に愛好される芸能として確立していきました。

　明治に入って絶大な人気を誇ったのが二代目松林伯円です。伯円（1834–1905）は「どろぼう伯円」の異名を取り、どろぼうの活躍する話を読むのを得意としました。彼は幕末の名優、四代目市川小団次の知遇を得て、河竹黙阿弥とも交際しました。伯円が作った「鼠小僧」や、河内山宗春が活躍する「天保六花

as street reciters, and thus the profession of *kōshakushi* (story-teller) was born.

These *kōshakushi* were respected as learned men and sometimes commissioned to recite war tales before the shōgun. During the Edo period, *kōdan* was taken more seriously than other arts such as *rakugo*, *manzai* (comic dialogue), and acrobatics, which tended to be viewed as light entertainment included to add variety.

 ## Who were the most eminent *kōshakushi*?

At a time when Edo society was becoming increasingly rigid, Fukai Shidōken was welcomed by the public as a satirical storyteller who went against the mainstream and criticized politics and society.

Active around the same time was Baba Bunkō, who become popular for reciting not only war tales but also stories about events and personalities of town society, including family troubles. Bunkō was censured and then executed by the shogunate for his criticism of politics. Nevertheless, Shidōken and Bunkō succeeded in establishing *kōdan* as an art loved by the ordinary public.

The most popular *kōshakushi* of the Meiji period was Matsubayashi Hakuen II (1834–1905), whose specialty was to recite the adventures of a thief, which earned him the name of "Hakuen the Thief." Hakuen enjoyed the favor of the celebrated kabuki actor Ichikawa Kodanji IV and was also on good terms with the kabuki dramatist Kawatake Mokuami. Mokuami dramatized stories by Hakuen such as *Nezumi Kozō*

撰」は、黙阿弥により歌舞伎化されています。

　幕末から明治にかけては、実在したやくざの清水次郎長を主人公にした「清水次郎長伝」や、「天保水滸伝」、「国定忠次」などが大衆の心をつかみ、多くの人気講釈師が出ました。

　講談は国立劇場演芸場、お江戸日本橋亭や、各地のホールでの独演会などで聞くことができます。

浪曲

Q　「浪曲」とはどんな芸能ですか。

　A　「浪花節」とも言います。講談とは違って、三味線を伴奏に、曲に乗って浪曲師が歌うように語る、語りの芸の1つです。江戸時代に、寺に属さない僧侶が仏教説話などを半ば踊りながら早口に歌って歩いたことが始まりと言われています。この歌を「ちょんがれ節」と言い、歌って歩いた僧侶を「ちょんがれ坊主」と言います。この「ちょんがれ」が、やがて三味線を伴奏とするようになり、上方で話芸として発達していきました。

　道端で人を集めて見せる大道芸だった「ちょんがれ」が、寄席に登場するようになったのは明治に入ってからで、そのころには「浪花節」と言われるようになりました。

and *Tenpō Rokkasen*, about the adventures of Kochiyama Sōshun.

From the end of the Tokugawa shogunate to the early Meiji period (1868–1912), stories such as *Shimizu Jirochōden*, about the real-life *yakuza* Shimizu no Jirochō, Tenpōsuikoden, and Kunisada Chūji, captured the public imagination and many popular storytellers appeared.

In addition to the regular performances at the Engeijō of the National Theater and the O-Edo Nihonbashitei, one-man performances of *kōdan* are given at various halls and theaters.

RŌKYOKU

 What kind of art is *rōkyoku*?

Rōkyoku, also commonly known as *naniwa-bushi*, is a narrative art which, unlike *kōdan*, is rhythmically intoned by a *rōkyokushi* (solo chanter) to the accompaniment of the shamisen. During the Edo period, itinerant priests not attached to a temple began the practice of rapidly chanting Buddhist tales while performing a sort of dance. This style of chanting was called *chongare-bushi* and the priests were known as *chongare-bōzu*. The narrative songs eventually came to be performed to the accompaniment of the shamisen and developed into a distinctive storytelling art in the Kyōto-Ōsaka region.

Chongare, which started out in this way as a form of street entertainment, was first performed at *yose* (*rakugo* theaters) in the Meiji period and came to be called *naniwa-bushi*.

「国定忠治」や「鼠小僧」などの講談の演目を取り入れて、これに節をつけた浪花節は、次第に大衆の人気を得るようになりました。

Q どんな人気浪曲師がいましたか。

桃中軒雲右衛門

A 明治時代に人気だったのは桃中軒雲右衛門（1873–1916）で、本郷座という劇場を約1ヵ月間も満員にしたほどです。レコードの普及が浪曲の人気に拍車をかけ、人々はその一節を口ずさみました。

広沢虎造

昭和に入って活躍した浪曲師には「清水次郎長伝」などを得意とした二代目広沢虎造（1899–1964）がいます。合間に軽妙な会話をはさんだ独特の節回しで、「虎造節」と言われました。
　浪曲は浪曲木馬亭や国立演芸場などで聞くことができます。

Stories usually performed in the *kōdan* style, such as *Kunisada Chūji* and *Nezumi Kozō*, were adapted to *naniwa-bushi* by adding intonation. These steadily grew in popularity.

 ## Who were the most popular *rōkyoku* performers?

One of the best loved *rōkyoku* performers in the Meiji period was Tōchūken Kumoemon (1873–1916), who drew a full house at the Hongō-za theater for a whole month. The popularization of the phonograph record in the early 1900s gave further impetus to the *rōkyoku* vogue, and people became so familiar with certain songs that they hummed or sang them to themselves.

A popular *rōkyoku* performer at the beginning of the Shōwa period (1926–1989) was Hirosawa Torazō (1899–1964), who was particularly well known for his rendition of stories such as *Shimizu Jirochō Den*. His unique style of inserting witty remarks in the intervals between verses was called Torazō-*bushi*.

Rōkyoku can be heard today at the Rōkyoku Mokubatei theater and the Engeijō of the National Theater.

日本語索引　JAPANESE INDEX

（「　」内は作品名）

英語で話す「日本の伝統芸能」
The Complete Guide to Traditional Japanese Performing Arts

2000 年 3 月 24 日　第 1 刷発行

著　者　　小玉祥子

発行者　　野間佐和子

発行所　　講談社インターナショナル株式会社
　　　　　〒112-8652　東京都文京区音羽 1-17-14
　　　　　電話：03-3944-6493（編集部）
　　　　　　　　03-3944-6492（業務部・営業部）

印刷所　　大日本印刷株式会社

製本所　　大日本印刷株式会社

落丁本、乱丁本は、講談社インターナショナル業務部宛にお送りください。送料小社負担にてお取替えいたします。なお、この本についてのお問い合わせは、編集部宛にお願いいたします。本書の無断複写（コピー）は著作権法上での例外を除き、禁じられています。

定価はカバーに表示してあります。

Copyright © 2000 Kodama Shōko.
ISBN4-7700-2607-2

対訳 英語で話す日本経済 Q & A
A Bilingual Guide to the Japanese Economy

NHK国際放送局経済プロジェクト・大和総研経済調査部 編　　ISBN 4-7700-1942-4
46判（128 x 188 mm）仮製　368ページ

NHK国際放送で好評を得た番組が本になりました。クイズと会話形式で楽しく読んでいくうちに、日本経済の仕組みが分かり、同時に英語にも強くなっていきます。日本語と英語の対応がひと目で分かる編集上の工夫もいっぱい。

対訳 おくのほそ道
The Narrow Road to Oku

松尾芭蕉 著　ドナルド・キーン 訳　宮田雅之 切り絵　　ISBN 4-7700-2028-7
A5判変型（140 x 226 mm）仮製 188ページ（カラー口絵41点）

古典文学の最高峰のひとつ「おくのほそ道」を、ドナルド・キーンが新訳しました。画家、宮田雅之が精魂を込めた切り絵の魅力とあいまって、この名作に新しい生命が吹き込まれた、必読の1冊です。

対訳 竹取物語
The Tale of the Bamboo Cutter

川端康成 現代語訳　ドナルド・キーン 英訳　宮田雅之 切り絵　　ISBN 4-7700-2329-4
A5判変型 横長（226 x 148 mm）仮製　箱入り　180ページ（カラー口絵16点）

ノーベル賞作家の現代語訳と傑出した芸術家の作品、そして日本文学の研究に一生を捧げたジャパノロジストの翻訳が合体した、大人のための「竹取物語」。

バイリンガル とってもかんたんマイレシピ
Stone Soup : Easy Japanese Home Cooking

渡辺節子 著　B5判変型（189 x 257 mm）仮製 256ページ　ISBN 4-7700-2061-9

手軽な日本の家庭料理、わが家の味160品目の作り方を英語と日本語で紹介したクッキングブック。作り方や調理器具などのイラスト付き、カロリー計算・調理時間もひと目で分かります。

対訳 日本事典
The Kodansha Bilingual Encyclopedia of Japan

講談社インターナショナル 編　　ISBN 4-7700-2130-5
B5判（182 x 257 mm）　上製　箱入り　944ページ（カラー口絵16ページ）

「日本」を国際的な視点で理解できる幅広い知識と、実用的な英語が身につきます。ビジネス、海外駐在、留学、ホームステイなど、さまざまな国際交流の場で、幅広くご活用いただけます。

- 現代の政治制度、最新の経済情報を豊富に記載し、日本を総合的に理解できる。
- 分野別の構成により、テーマに沿って自然に読み進むことができる。
- 豊富なイラストと図版を収録し、完全対訳のレイアウトと欄外のキーワードで、重要単語や表現の日英相互参照に便利。
- 日本国憲法、重要な国際条約、年表をいずれも日英併記で巻末に収録。
- 英語からも日本語（ローマ字）からも引けるインデックスつき。

内容構成：地理 / 歴史 / 政治 / 経済 / 社会 / 文化 / 生活

講談社バイリンガル・ブックス （オン・カセット/オンCD）英語で聞いても面白い!

🔊 印のタイトルは、英文テキスト部分を録音したカセット・テープが、また 💿 印のタイトルは英文テキスト部分を録音したCDが発売されています。本との併用により聞く力・話す力を高め、実用的な英語が身につく格好のリスニング教材です。

講談社パワー・イングリッシュ

実用英語の総合シリーズ

- 旅行・留学からビジネスまで、コミュニケーションの現場で役立つ「実用性」
- ニューヨーク、ロンドンの各拠点での、ネイティブ チェックにより保証される「信頼性」
- 英語の主要ジャンルを網羅し、目的に応じた本選びができる「総合性」

46判変型（113 x 188 mm）仮製

---

1 これを英語で言えますか？　学校で教えてくれない身近な英単語

講談社インターナショナル 編　　　　　　　　232ページ　ISBN 4-7700-2132-1

「ブランコ、鉄棒、すべり台」「短縮ダイヤル」「○×式テスト」「$a^2 + b^3 = c^4$」「円の面積はπ掛ける半径の2乗」「いない、いない、ばー」…これらを英語で言えますか？　本書は日本人英語の盲点に77の分野から迫ります。

---

2 遠山顕の英会話・150のスパイス　ムリなく使える決まり文句

遠山　顕 著　　　　　　　　　　　　　　　240ページ　ISBN 4-7700-2586-6
　　　　　　　　　　　　　　　CD（70分×1枚）別売　ISBN 4-7700-2587-4

「一杯いこうか？」「なるようになりますよ」「テコでも動きませんよ」など、欧米人の会話にもしばしば使われる決まり文句150を、"やさしい""短い"をポイントに、選りすぐって紹介。すべて具体的な用例付きで応用も自由自在の、会話のスパイス集。（CD別売）

---

3 アメリカ旅行「使える」キーワード　場面別想定問答集

アンドリュー・ホルバート 著　　　　　　　240ページ　ISBN 4-7700-2481-9

出国から帰国まで、アメリカ旅行のすべてをカバーする一冊。ショッピングや食事、レンタカーの借り方からトラブル対処法まで様々な状況で必要となる決め手のフレーズ。そんな「コトバ」と、初心者でも楽しく旅ができる実用的な「情報」を満載。

---

4 ダメ！ その英語［ビジネス編］　日本人英語NG集

連東孝子 著　　　　　　　　　　　　　　　176ページ　ISBN 4-7700-2469-X

社長賞を貰ったアメリカ人の同僚に "You are lucky!" と言ってはダメ!?　ビジネスの場面を中心に、コミュニケーションの行き違い110例を紹介・解説。「この英語、なぜいけないの？」「この表現がどうして通じないの？」に答える、日本人英語のウィークポイント攻略本。

---

5 米語イディオム600　ELTで学ぶ使い分け&言い替え

バーバラ・ゲインズ 著　　　　　　　　　　208ページ　ISBN 4-7700-2461-4

イディオムを使いこなせるかどうかが英会話上達の決め手!　本書は「勘定を払う」「仕事を探す」など、日常生活に即した80の場面別に600以上の重要イディオムを紹介。ただ機械的に暗記するのではなく、状況に応じた言い替え・使い分けがマスターできる。

---

6 どこまで使える？ "go" と "come"　かんたん単語55の英会話

田崎清忠 著　　　　　　　　　　　　　　　208ページ　ISBN 4-7700-2527-0

"come" "take" "leave" など、中学校で習う初歩的な単語も、使い方次第で表現力が大幅アップ！　誰もが知っている簡単な単語55の意味と使い方を、肩の凝らないエッセイを通して紹介。つい見落としがちな、意味と用法の意外なバリエーションが気軽に学べる。

7 アメリカ留学日常語事典　これがなければ1日も過ごせない!

東 照二 著　　　　　　　　　　192ページ　ISBN 4-7700-2470-3

アメリカのキャンパスには、独特の用語や表現がいっぱいあります。本書は、留学を志す人、アメリカのキャンパスで生活する人が知っていないと困る用語と情報を一挙にまとめて、日本人にわかりやすく解説しました。

8 マナー違反の英会話　英語にだって「敬語」があります

ジェームス・M・バーダマン、森本豊富 共著　　　　208ページ　ISBN 4-7700-2520-3

英語にだって「敬語」はあります。「アメリカ人はフランクで開放的」と言われていますが、お互いを傷つけないように非常に気配りをしています。しかし親しい仲間うちで丁寧な英語表現ばかりを使っていては、打ち解けられません。英語にだってTPOがあります。場に応じた英語表現を使い分けましょう。

9 英語で「四字熟語」365　英語にするとこんなにカンタン!

松野守峰、N・ミナイ 共著　　　　　272ページ　ISBN 4-7700-2466-5

四字熟語をマスターし、その英語表現によってボキャブラリーも急増する一石二鳥のおトクな1冊!　日常よく使われる365の四字熟語を「努力・忍耐」「リーダーシップ」「チームワーク」「苦境」「性格」「能力」「友情」「恋愛」「宿命」などの意味別に分類し、英語にしました。

10 「英語モード」で英会話　これがネイティブの発想法

脇山 怜、佐野キム・マリー 共著　　　　224ページ　ISBN 4-7700-2522-X

英語でコミュニケーションをするときは、日本語から英語へ、「モード」のスイッチを切り替えましょう。日本では、へりくだって相手を持ち上げることが、処世術とされています。ところが、「未経験で何もわからませんがよろしく」のつもりで "I am inexperienced and I don't know anything." なんて英語圏で言えば、それはマイナスイメージ。「日本語モード」の英語は誤解のもとです。

11 英語で読む「科学ニュース」　話題の知識を英語でGet!

松野守峰 著　　　　　　　　　　208ページ　ISBN 4-7700-2456-8

科学に関する知識とことばが同時に身につく、画期的な英語実用書!「ネット恐怖症候群」「スマート・マウスパッド」から「デザイナー・ドラッグ」「DNAによる全人類の祖先解明」まで、いま話題の科学情報が英語でスラスラ読めるようになります。ていねいな語句解説と豊富な用語リストにより、ボキャブラリーも大幅アップ!

12 CDブック 英会話・ぜったい・音読　頭の中に英語回路を作る本

國弘正雄 編　千田潤一 トレーニング指導　　　144ページ　CD（40分×1枚）付
　　　　　　　　　　　　　　　　　　　　　　　　ISBN 4-7700-2459-2

英語を身につけるには、英語の基礎回路を作ることが先決です。英語を身体で覚える…、それには、何と言っても音読です。本書には、中学3年生用の文部省検定済み英語教科書7冊から、成人の英語トレーニングに適した12レッスンを厳選して収録しました。だまされたと思って、まずは3ヵ月続けてみてください。確かな身体の変化にきっと驚かれることでしょう。

13 英語のサインを読む　アメリカ生活情報早わかりマニュアル

清地恵美子 著　　　　　　　　　　240ページ　ISBN 4-7700-2519-X

広告や看板の読み方がわかると、アメリカの英語と暮らしが見えてきます。「スーパーのチラシに$2.99Lb.とあるけど意味がわからない」、「コインランドリーを使いたいのだけれど」、「駐車場の出口で料金の支払い方がわからないので、出られない!」…、そんな時に限って、周りにだれもいないものです。本書では自動販売機の使い方、案内板や利用説明書の読み方など、生活情報入手のコツを28分野にわたって紹介しました。

あなたの英語が変わる

講談社パワー・イングリッシュ

ネイティブチェック済

これを英語で言えますか？

学校で教えてくれない身近な英単語

四捨五入する	round off
5^2	five squared
モーニングコール	wake-up call
ホチキス	stapler
昇進	promotion
協調介入	coordinated intervention
貸し渋り	credit crunch
介護保険	nursing care insurance
花粉症	hay fever
朝飯前だよ	That's a piece of cake!

講談社インターナショナル 編
232ページ
ISBN 4-7700-2132-1

日本人英語の盲点になっている英単語に、78のジャンルから迫ります。
読んでみれば、「なーんだ、こんなやさしい単語だったのか」、「そうか、こう言えば良かったのか」と思いあたる単語や表現がいっぱいです。
雑学も満載しましたので、忘れていた単語が生き返ってくるだけでなく、覚えたことが記憶に残ります。弱点克服のボキャビルに最適です。